Circular Energy Economy for a Sustainable Future: Advancing Renewable Energy, Energy Efficiency, Green Technology, Resource Recovery, Digitalization, and Climate Resilience

Copyright

Circular Energy Economy for a Sustainable Future: Advancing Renewable Energy, Energy Efficiency, Green Technology, Resource Recovery, Digitalization, and Climate Resilience

© 2025 Robert C. Brears

The author and publisher are of the same opinion regarding the views and content expressed in this work.

Disclaimer: The information in this book is provided for general knowledge and educational purposes only. While every effort has been made to ensure accuracy, the author and publisher make no representations or warranties with respect to the completeness or suitability of the content. The author and publisher accept no liability for any errors, omissions, or outcomes resulting from the application of information contained herein. Readers are advised to consult appropriate professionals or authorities before acting on any material presented.

ISBN (eBook): **978-1-991368-55-3**

ISBN (Paperback): **978-1-991368-56-0**

Published by Global Climate Solutions

First Edition, 2025

Cover design and interior layout by Global Climate Solutions

Table of Contents

Introduction

The transition to a circular energy economy marks a profound shift in how societies produce, distribute, and consume energy. It challenges the traditional linear model—based on extraction, use, and disposal—that has long dominated industrial and economic development. Instead, it promotes a regenerative system in which energy production and resource use are optimized, waste is minimized, and materials are continuously cycled back into productive use. This transformation is driven by the urgent need to address global challenges such as climate change, resource scarcity, and environmental degradation, while ensuring economic resilience and social equity.

A circular energy economy builds upon the principles of the broader circular economy but focuses specifically on the energy system as both a driver and enabler of sustainability. It integrates renewable energy sources, resource efficiency, and technological innovation into cohesive frameworks that reduce dependency on finite resources and mitigate greenhouse gas emissions. Unlike conventional energy systems that rely heavily on fossil fuels, the circular model emphasizes renewable generation—such as solar, wind, and geothermal energy—supported by closed-loop material cycles, advanced storage solutions, and intelligent management systems. This approach not only decarbonizes energy supply but also strengthens energy security and enhances the resilience of infrastructure and communities.

At its core, the circular energy economy recognizes the interconnectedness of energy with materials, water, and ecosystems. Every stage of the energy value chain—from extraction and production to consumption and end-of-life management—presents opportunities to reduce waste, recover resources, and improve efficiency. Technologies such as waste-to-energy conversion, battery recycling, and digital optimization enable systems to operate more efficiently and sustainably. When combined with supportive policy frameworks, financial instruments, and social innovation, these measures create an integrated system that aligns economic growth with environmental regeneration.

Governance and institutional frameworks play a critical role in shaping circular energy transitions. Effective coordination across national, regional, and local levels ensures that energy systems evolve coherently and inclusively. Public-private partnerships, regulatory innovation, and collaborative financing mechanisms provide the foundation for scaling circular solutions. At the same time, education, awareness, and cultural change are essential to ensure broad public participation and acceptance. Circular transitions depend on shared understanding and engagement, transforming consumers into active participants and innovators within the system.

Digitalization accelerates this transformation by providing the intelligence required for real-time optimization and decision-making. Artificial intelligence, the Internet of Things, and blockchain technologies enable transparency, traceability, and predictive management across energy value chains. These tools connect generation, distribution, and consumption into a dynamic, adaptive network that continuously learns and evolves. By integrating data-driven insights with circular design principles, digital technologies make it possible to close resource loops and enhance system-wide performance.

The circular energy economy represents not just an environmental or technological shift, but a systemic rethinking of how societies organize production and consumption. It aims to balance the demands of economic development with the limits of the planet's resources, creating a pathway toward resilience, equity, and long-term sustainability. This book explores the key principles, systems, and strategies underpinning this transformation—from renewable integration and efficiency optimization to governance frameworks and social innovation. Through this exploration, it seeks to provide a comprehensive understanding of how circular energy systems can power a regenerative, low-carbon future.

Chapter 1: Foundations of the Circular Energy Economy

The foundations of the circular energy economy lie in redefining how societies view and manage energy systems. Moving away from linear models of extraction and waste, circular approaches emphasize regeneration, efficiency, and closed-loop processes. This chapter introduces the conceptual basis of circularity in the energy context, explaining how renewable resources, system integration, and technological innovation interact to form resilient energy systems. It explores the principles of resource efficiency, systems thinking, and lifecycle design while tracing the historical evolution toward circularity. Together, these elements establish the intellectual and practical framework for a sustainable, regenerative energy future.

Defining the Circular Energy Economy

The circular energy economy represents a transformative shift in how societies produce, distribute, and consume energy. Unlike the traditional linear model—where energy systems follow a "take, make, dispose" trajectory—the circular model emphasizes regeneration, reuse, and continual optimization of resources. In a circular framework, energy generation, infrastructure, and consumption are designed to create closed loops, where waste and inefficiency are systematically reduced or eliminated. This approach aligns with the broader principles of the circular economy, applying them specifically to the energy sector to ensure that resources remain in circulation for as long as possible while minimizing environmental impacts.

At its foundation, the circular energy economy seeks to decouple economic growth from resource depletion. Traditional energy systems rely heavily on the extraction and combustion of fossil fuels, leading to emissions, waste heat, and discarded materials that cannot be easily reused. The circular model reverses this pattern by integrating renewable energy sources—such as solar, wind, hydro, and bioenergy—within systems that maximize efficiency and recovery. Energy production becomes regenerative rather than extractive, as renewable technologies operate in harmony with natural cycles. Moreover, energy infrastructures are designed for longevity, flexibility, and adaptability, allowing components to be repurposed or upgraded rather than discarded.

A defining feature of the circular energy economy is its focus on material and energy symbiosis. In practice, this means that by-products from one process can serve as inputs for another, creating self-reinforcing loops across sectors. For example, waste heat from industrial operations can be captured and reused for district heating, while organic waste can be converted into biogas or biofuels to power transportation and manufacturing. Through such interconnections, the boundaries between production and consumption blur, fostering a dynamic system that optimizes resource flows across industries and communities.

Digital technologies play a central role in enabling this transition. Smart grids, artificial intelligence, and data analytics facilitate real-time monitoring and management of energy flows, allowing supply and demand to be balanced efficiently. Blockchain enhances transparency in energy trading and certification, ensuring accountability and trust in decentralized systems. Meanwhile, the Internet of Things (IoT) allows buildings, vehicles, and appliances to communicate, coordinating consumption patterns to reduce waste and improve performance. Together, these tools support the integration of diverse energy sources, enhance grid stability, and accelerate the feedback loops essential for circularity.

The circular energy economy also extends beyond technology to encompass social and institutional innovation. It redefines relationships among producers, consumers, and policymakers, transforming consumers into active participants—prosumers—who generate, store, and share energy within local networks. Governance structures evolve toward collaboration and inclusivity, where decisions about energy use and investment incorporate environmental, social, and economic considerations. Communities, businesses, and governments work together to design systems that serve long-term societal goals, including climate mitigation, energy security, and equitable access.

Crucially, this model reframes waste not as an inevitable by-product but as a valuable resource. Whether it is waste energy, materials, or emissions, circular thinking transforms inefficiencies into opportunities for regeneration. For instance, carbon capture and utilization technologies convert emissions into new materials, while recycling of components in solar panels or batteries reduces the demand for virgin resources. These processes not only conserve materials but also lower lifecycle emissions, reinforcing the connection between circularity and decarbonization.

The defining characteristic of the circular energy economy, therefore, lies in its systemic nature. It moves beyond isolated improvements in efficiency toward the complete redesign of energy systems to function within planetary boundaries. By linking renewable energy expansion, resource recovery, and sustainable consumption patterns, the circular energy economy creates pathways for resilient and regenerative growth. It represents not merely a technological evolution but a paradigm shift in how societies conceive and manage energy—a framework that aligns human progress with ecological balance and long-term sustainability.

Key Principles and Systemic Thinking

The circular energy economy is grounded in core principles that reshape how energy is generated, distributed, and consumed. These principles—resource efficiency, regeneration, and closed-loop systems—are interconnected through systems thinking, which provides a holistic framework for managing energy flows and dependencies across sectors.

Resource efficiency focuses on maximizing the value derived from every unit of energy and material throughout its life cycle. It emphasizes reducing losses at each stage of production, transmission, and consumption while maintaining service quality and reliability. Efficient energy systems lower input demands and emissions, helping to alleviate pressure on finite resources. Technological innovations such as advanced monitoring, automation, and real-time energy analytics enhance this process, allowing continuous improvement rather than one-time optimization.

Regeneration centers on replenishing and restoring natural systems that sustain energy production. Renewable sources such as solar, wind, and hydropower inherently follow regenerative cycles, providing energy without depleting underlying resources. Regeneration also includes rehabilitating ecosystems impacted by energy infrastructure, such as restoring wetlands affected by hydropower or reforesting areas used for bioenergy production. This approach ensures that energy systems maintain balance with ecological processes, contributing to environmental resilience and long-term resource stability.

Closed-loop systems maintain materials and energy within circulation, preventing waste and reducing dependency on new extraction. In practice, this involves designing processes where one operation's output serves as another's input. Examples include using excess industrial heat in district heating, converting organic waste into bioenergy, or recycling materials from decommissioned solar panels and wind turbines. These feedback loops extend product life cycles, conserve critical resources, and support the transition toward more autonomous and efficient energy systems.

Systems thinking provides the integrative framework that connects these principles. It views the energy economy as an interconnected network of processes, where actions in one domain affect others through dynamic relationships. This perspective encourages cross-sector coordination and foresight, recognizing that renewable expansion, material use, and consumer behavior influence one another. Systems thinking highlights feedback mechanisms, trade-offs, and opportunities for synergy across technological, environmental, and social dimensions.

Applying systems thinking to energy management enables coherent strategies that reflect the complexity of real-world systems. Rather than focusing on isolated technological improvements, it promotes integrated approaches where renewable deployment aligns with circular manufacturing, urban planning, and digital innovation. Coordinated policies and adaptive governance structures emerge from this mindset, supporting balanced progress toward sustainability, efficiency, and resilience.

The combination of these principles under a systems-thinking framework creates an adaptive and interconnected foundation for the circular energy economy. It ensures that energy transitions are not only technologically advanced but also resource-conscious, regenerative, and aligned with the broader functioning of natural and human systems.

The Energy-Resource Nexus

The relationship between energy and resources is deeply intertwined, forming the foundation of modern economies and societies. The extraction, processing, and transportation of materials depend heavily on energy inputs, while energy production itself requires vast quantities of water, minerals, land, and other natural resources. This mutual dependency creates a complex web known as the energy-resource nexus. Understanding and managing this nexus is essential to achieving sustainability, as inefficiencies or disruptions in one system can rapidly cascade through others.

In a traditional linear economy, energy and resource flows are treated as separate systems. Energy production often relies on non-renewable resources that are extracted, used, and ultimately discarded, while materials are consumed in a similar one-way path from source to waste. This approach leads to high levels of environmental degradation, resource depletion, and greenhouse gas emissions. It also increases vulnerability to supply disruptions and market volatility, particularly for countries dependent on imported energy or critical materials. A circular approach redefines this relationship, seeking to align energy and material flows within regenerative cycles that reduce waste and enhance resilience.

The circular energy economy addresses the nexus by promoting the efficient use and reuse of both energy and materials. For example, renewable energy technologies such as solar panels and wind turbines require metals and minerals, yet circular principles ensure these resources are reused through recycling and recovery at the end of their life cycles. Likewise, circularity in energy systems emphasizes the recovery of by-products—such as heat, gases, or organic waste—that would otherwise be lost. These feedback mechanisms minimize pressure on ecosystems and lower the demand for virgin resource extraction.

Energy production also has significant implications for water and land use. Conventional power generation, particularly fossil fuel and nuclear plants, consumes large volumes of water for cooling and extraction processes. In contrast, renewable energy systems typically use less water and can be designed to integrate with other land uses, such as agriculture or urban development. For instance, agrivoltaic systems allow solar panels to coexist with crops, optimizing both energy generation and food production. Similarly, offshore wind farms can coexist with marine ecosystems and fisheries when designed with ecological sensitivity. By integrating such multifunctional approaches, circular energy systems reduce competition for resources and enhance environmental co-benefits.

The material intensity of renewable technologies requires careful management to avoid shifting environmental burdens from one domain to another. A circular strategy mitigates this risk by promoting responsible sourcing, modular design, and end-of-life recovery. This involves designing components that are easy to disassemble, repair, or recycle, ensuring that valuable materials remain in circulation. In addition, the use of alternative or bio-based materials can reduce dependency on finite mineral reserves. The integration of digital tracking technologies, such as blockchain and product passports, supports transparency in supply chains and enables efficient resource management across production cycles.

Urban and industrial systems also play a key role in closing energy and resource loops. Industrial symbiosis, where one facility's waste or by-product becomes another's input, exemplifies how circularity operates at the nexus. Waste heat from manufacturing can be captured and distributed through district heating networks, while organic waste can be converted into bioenergy. In cities, circular energy practices include the reuse of treated wastewater for cooling and power generation, or the recovery of materials from demolished infrastructure to construct new buildings. These integrated approaches not only reduce waste and emissions but also create localized resource security.

The energy-resource nexus extends to consumption patterns and societal behavior. Efficient product design, shared ownership models, and shifts toward renewable-powered mobility systems all reduce the material and energy intensity of daily life. Encouraging consumers to participate in decentralized energy systems—such as community solar or peer-to-peer energy trading—builds awareness of resource interconnections and promotes collective responsibility.

Managing the energy-resource nexus through circular principles also enhances resilience to global shocks. Systems that depend less on imported fuels or raw materials are less exposed to geopolitical risks and price fluctuations. Circularity builds adaptive capacity by diversifying energy sources, extending material lifespans, and creating feedback systems that adjust to changing conditions. These characteristics are critical for societies facing climate-related disruptions, resource scarcity, and population growth.

The energy-resource nexus demonstrates that sustainability cannot be achieved through isolated interventions. Circularity provides the structure to harmonize energy and material use, transforming interdependence into a source of strength rather than vulnerability. Through systemic coordination and continuous regeneration, the circular energy economy aligns the flow of resources with ecological limits while maintaining the foundations of prosperity and stability.

Historical Evolution Toward Circularity

The evolution of circular concepts within energy systems has unfolded gradually over more than a century, shaped by technological innovation, policy shifts, and changing societal values. Early industrial systems operated on a linear model of energy and resource use, emphasizing extraction, production, and consumption with little regard for long-term environmental or material consequences. Over time, awareness of finite resources and ecological limits spurred new thinking on efficiency, conservation, and regeneration. These ideas laid the groundwork for today's circular energy economy, which integrates renewable energy, resource recovery, and systemic design.

In the late nineteenth and early twentieth centuries, industrial growth relied heavily on coal, oil, and gas. Energy systems were designed for abundance and expansion, not for sustainability. Efficiency improvements during this period were motivated primarily by economic gains rather than environmental stewardship. Steam engines, electricity generation, and manufacturing processes evolved to maximize output per unit of fuel, driven by industrial competition. However, these efforts remained confined within a linear framework, where materials and energy were used once and discarded. The concept of waste as a resource had not yet entered mainstream thought.

The mid-twentieth century marked a turning point. Rapid post-war industrialization and population growth led to rising resource consumption and pollution. The 1970s oil crises revealed the vulnerability of energy systems dependent on finite fossil fuels and external suppliers. Governments and industries began to emphasize energy conservation and diversification as strategic priorities. Efficiency programs emerged across sectors, including building insulation standards, fuel economy regulations, and the development of cogeneration technologies that utilized waste heat for industrial and district heating. These developments reflected the early stages of a more integrated understanding of energy use and resource management.

At the same time, environmental awareness grew through global movements and landmark events such as the publication of *The Limits to Growth* in 1972 and the establishment of international environmental agreements. Concepts such as sustainable development and ecological economics began to influence energy policy and research. Energy systems were increasingly evaluated not only for their economic performance but also for their environmental impacts. This shift introduced life-cycle thinking, encouraging assessment of energy technologies from production through disposal. Although circularity as a defined framework had not yet emerged, the principles of resource efficiency and environmental responsibility were gaining institutional recognition.

The late twentieth century saw the rise of renewable energy technologies as viable alternatives to fossil fuels. Advances in solar photovoltaics, wind power, and bioenergy shifted energy discussions from extraction to regeneration. These technologies embodied circular principles by harnessing naturally replenishing flows rather than depleting finite stocks. The expansion of renewable energy also stimulated innovation in energy storage, smart grids, and demand-side management—tools that improved system flexibility and efficiency. During this period, recycling and material recovery in industrial processes also gained traction, reinforcing the broader idea that waste could be reintegrated into productive cycles.

By the early twenty-first century, the circular economy framework began to take shape as an explicit model for sustainable development. Its principles—reduce, reuse, recycle, recover, and regenerate—provided a cohesive structure for linking material and energy systems. In the energy sector, this translated into strategies for optimizing resource use across entire value chains. Policies promoting renewable energy integration, energy efficiency, and low-carbon transitions were increasingly viewed through a circular lens. The rise of the European Union's Circular Economy Action Plan and similar initiatives globally underscored the political recognition of circularity as essential to climate and energy goals.

Digitalization further accelerated this transition. Technologies such as smart meters, artificial intelligence, and blockchain introduced new capabilities for monitoring and optimizing energy systems. Real-time data made it possible to align production with consumption, manage grid stability, and enhance transparency in resource flows. These innovations created feedback mechanisms—hallmarks of circular systems—that continuously improved performance while reducing waste.

Today's circular energy economy builds on decades of evolution, combining the lessons of efficiency movements with the regenerative potential of renewables and digital systems. It represents the culmination of a historical shift from linear resource exploitation toward integrated, adaptive, and restorative models. Circularity in energy is not a sudden invention but the result of a continuous process of learning and innovation, driven by the recognition that sustainable prosperity depends on harmonizing economic activity with ecological and material boundaries.

Chapter 2: Renewable Energy as the Cornerstone of Circularity

Renewable energy lies at the heart of the circular energy economy, providing the foundation for a sustainable and regenerative energy system. By replacing finite fossil fuels with abundant, low-carbon sources such as solar, wind, hydro, and geothermal power, renewables decouple growth from resource depletion. This chapter explores how renewable energy enables circularity through its integration into industrial, urban, and digital systems. It examines strategies for overcoming variability, enhancing storage, and linking renewables to resource efficiency. Together, these elements illustrate how renewable energy not only drives decarbonization but also anchors long-term resilience and circular resource management.

Expanding the Role of Renewable Energy

Renewable energy forms the foundation of the circular energy economy by breaking the dependency between energy generation and finite resource consumption. Unlike fossil fuels, which are extracted and depleted through linear use, renewables draw on natural flows that replenish continuously—solar radiation, wind currents, hydrological cycles, and geothermal heat. This regenerative quality positions renewables as the core enabler of circularity, providing a sustainable supply of energy that supports closed-loop systems and long-term resilience.

The shift toward renewable energy represents more than a technological transition; it signifies a reorientation of economic and environmental systems. Fossil fuel-based models rely on continuous extraction and combustion, leading to emissions, waste, and resource loss. Renewable systems, in contrast, rely on inputs that are part of Earth's natural cycles, eliminating the depletion of stocks while reducing pollution and carbon emissions. This shift decouples economic growth from fossil fuel dependence and environmental degradation, enabling societies to sustain development within ecological limits.

Renewable energy's integration into the circular economy framework is not limited to generation. It influences how energy is distributed, stored, and consumed. By coupling renewable generation with technologies such as battery storage, hydrogen production, and demand-response systems, circular models ensure that clean energy remains available when and where it is needed. These systems help stabilize grids with high shares of variable renewables, reducing reliance on backup fossil capacity and supporting continuous, low-emission energy flows.

Circularity in renewable energy systems also extends to their design and material use. Renewable technologies require metals, minerals, and composite materials that must be managed responsibly to prevent new forms of resource depletion. Circular design principles address this challenge by emphasizing durability, modularity, and recyclability. Components such as solar panels, wind turbine blades, and batteries can be designed for easy disassembly and material recovery. End-of-life recycling programs, combined with innovations in material substitution, ensure that renewable infrastructure contributes to resource efficiency rather than creating future waste streams.

The decentralization of renewable energy aligns closely with circular principles by empowering communities and industries to produce and manage energy locally. Distributed renewable systems—such as rooftop solar, small-scale wind, and biogas units—enable energy generation close to demand centers, minimizing transmission losses and strengthening resilience. Localized systems support prosumer participation, where consumers become active producers and managers of energy. This not only diversifies supply but also fosters social and economic inclusion, as communities retain greater control over their energy resources.

Renewables also facilitate sectoral integration, allowing the coupling of electricity with transport, heating, cooling, and industrial processes. Electrification of end-use sectors powered by renewables enhances energy efficiency and enables circularity across broader systems. For example, electric vehicles powered by renewable energy contribute to reducing emissions while their batteries can later serve in stationary storage applications. Similarly, renewable electricity can be used to produce green hydrogen, which can substitute fossil fuels in hard-to-abate sectors such as steelmaking and shipping. This interconnectedness creates feedback loops where renewable energy acts as the driving force behind multiple forms of circular transformation.

Beyond technological benefits, renewable energy supports environmental regeneration. The displacement of fossil fuels reduces air pollution, limits water consumption, and minimizes habitat destruction associated with mining and drilling. Properly planned renewable projects can coexist with ecosystems and other land uses through thoughtful siting and design. Offshore wind farms, for example, can support marine biodiversity when designed with ecological considerations. Solar farms can be integrated into agricultural systems, enhancing both energy and food production. These multifunctional landscapes embody the circular principle of maximizing the value and productivity of each resource.

The economic implications of expanding renewables are equally significant. As technologies mature and costs decline, renewables are becoming the most competitive sources of new power generation in many regions. Their scalability allows both advanced and developing economies to transition toward cleaner energy while stimulating green industries, job creation, and innovation. Investment in renewables drives economic diversification, reduces exposure to fossil fuel volatility, and aligns national development pathways with global climate goals.

Renewable energy thus represents the cornerstone of the circular energy economy. It transforms the way societies generate and use energy by replacing finite extraction with perpetual regeneration. Through careful design, responsible material management, and systemic integration, renewables enable economies to operate within environmental boundaries while ensuring stable, equitable access to energy.

Integrating Renewable Energy into Industrial and Urban Systems

Integrating renewable energy into industrial and urban systems is central to advancing the circular energy economy. Both settings consume large amounts of energy and materials, making them critical arenas for embedding renewable technologies that reduce emissions, close resource loops, and enhance efficiency. By redesigning how cities and industries generate and manage energy, societies can transform traditionally linear systems into dynamic, regenerative networks that support sustainable growth.

In industrial systems, renewable energy integration begins with the substitution of fossil fuels with clean power sources. Manufacturing processes that rely on thermal energy, electricity, or mechanical work can be powered by solar, wind, hydro, or bioenergy, significantly lowering their carbon intensity. Industrial parks and clusters can adopt shared renewable infrastructure, where multiple facilities benefit from centralized renewable generation combined with storage and waste recovery. For example, integrating rooftop solar panels or on-site wind turbines can meet a substantial share of electricity demand, while bioenergy plants convert waste from nearby industries into power or heat. These arrangements foster industrial symbiosis, where energy and material flows between companies become more efficient and mutually reinforcing.

Renewable integration in industry also requires a rethinking of production processes to accommodate fluctuating supply. Many renewable sources, such as solar and wind, are intermittent. To adapt, industries employ demand flexibility strategies, aligning production schedules with periods of abundant renewable generation. Energy storage systems—batteries, thermal storage, and hydrogen—help smooth fluctuations and ensure reliability. Digitalization enhances this adaptability by using real-time data analytics and predictive algorithms to coordinate energy supply and demand across complex operations. The result is a responsive industrial ecosystem capable of maintaining productivity while minimizing waste and energy loss.

In urban systems, renewable energy integration transforms cities from passive consumers into active energy ecosystems. Urban areas concentrate population, infrastructure, and economic activity, making them both major energy users and potential producers. Rooftop solar installations, small-scale wind systems, and waste-to-energy facilities allow cities to generate clean energy locally. This distributed generation model reduces dependence on centralized grids and transmission networks, improving resilience during disruptions. Coupled with smart grid technology, cities can manage energy flows dynamically, balancing generation, consumption, and storage across neighborhoods.

Urban design plays an essential role in facilitating renewable energy integration. Buildings can be constructed or retrofitted to function as energy-efficient micro-hubs that produce, store, and share energy. Building-integrated photovoltaics, green roofs, and passive design features reduce energy consumption while supporting decentralized generation. District heating and cooling networks powered by geothermal or solar thermal systems further optimize urban energy use by redistributing waste heat and renewable thermal energy across sectors. By linking energy, water, and waste systems through shared infrastructure, cities achieve higher efficiency and reduce environmental impacts.

The service sector also benefits from renewable energy integration. Offices, schools, hospitals, and commercial centers are adopting on-site renewables and energy-efficient technologies to lower operational costs and carbon footprints. The digital economy's expansion has increased energy demand in data centers and communication networks, but renewable integration mitigates this impact. Data centers increasingly operate on 100 percent renewable power and use waste heat for nearby facilities, illustrating how service-based operations can contribute to resource circularity.

Integrating renewables into transportation systems complements industrial and urban transformations. Electrification of mobility, supported by renewable-powered grids, reduces dependence on petroleum-based fuels. Public transport fleets, electric vehicle charging infrastructure, and logistics hubs powered by renewables enhance urban air quality and reduce lifecycle emissions. When connected with renewable microgrids, these systems can operate flexibly and support grid stability by providing distributed storage capacity.

Governance and policy frameworks play a decisive role in enabling integration across sectors. Municipal governments can facilitate renewable adoption through zoning regulations, green building standards, and incentives for distributed generation. Industrial policy can encourage collaborative investment in shared renewable assets and support innovation in clean technologies. Cross-sector partnerships between utilities, manufacturers, and urban planners are essential for coordinating resource flows and aligning infrastructure development with sustainability goals.

Integrating renewable energy into industrial and urban systems creates interconnected networks that recycle resources, recover energy, and reduce waste. The result is a transformation from isolated, resource-intensive operations into self-sustaining systems that reinforce one another. By embedding renewables into the physical and functional fabric of cities and industries, the circular energy economy moves closer to achieving resilience, efficiency, and balance between economic activity and environmental integrity.

Overcoming Variability and Storage Challenges

Managing the variability of renewable energy is one of the central challenges in creating a stable and resilient circular energy economy. Solar and wind power, while clean and abundant, fluctuate with weather and time, leading to mismatches between supply and demand. Addressing this intermittency requires a combination of technical, economic, and policy solutions that enhance grid flexibility, expand storage capacity, and integrate diverse energy resources into cohesive systems.

Flexible grid systems are the backbone of renewable integration. Modern grids must accommodate a mix of centralized and decentralized generation sources while maintaining reliability. Smart grid technologies enable this flexibility by using real-time data and automated controls to balance generation and consumption. Sensors, advanced metering, and predictive analytics allow operators to anticipate fluctuations in renewable output and adjust system operations accordingly. Demand-side management programs complement these tools by shifting consumption to periods of high renewable availability. For example, electric vehicle charging, industrial processes, and household appliances can be programmed to operate when solar or wind generation peaks, reducing strain on the grid.

Energy storage plays an equally vital role in overcoming renewable variability. Storage systems bridge temporal gaps between production and demand, ensuring energy is available when generation is low. Batteries are currently the most widely deployed storage technology due to their scalability and responsiveness. Lithium-ion batteries, in particular, have become essential components of renewable systems, providing frequency regulation and short-term balancing. Emerging technologies, such as solid-state batteries and flow batteries, promise longer lifespans, safer operation, and greater sustainability through improved recyclability.

Beyond batteries, other storage technologies address different temporal and spatial scales. Pumped hydro storage, one of the oldest and most mature methods, remains the dominant form of large-scale energy storage, capable of storing energy over days or weeks. Compressed air and thermal energy storage systems complement these by converting surplus electricity into alternative energy forms for later use. Hydrogen storage represents another promising pathway: surplus renewable energy can power electrolysis to produce hydrogen, which can then be stored, transported, and converted back into electricity or used directly in industry and transport. Together, these storage solutions enhance energy system resilience and reduce dependence on fossil fuel-based backup generation.

Decentralized energy systems further mitigate variability by diversifying generation and enhancing local reliability. Microgrids and community-scale renewable systems can operate independently during grid disturbances, using a combination of solar panels, small wind turbines, and on-site storage. These systems strengthen energy security and reduce transmission losses while enabling localized resource optimization. Peer-to-peer energy trading platforms, supported by blockchain technology, facilitate energy exchange among prosumers, allowing surplus renewable power to be shared or sold within local networks.

Policy and regulatory frameworks are essential for accelerating storage deployment and grid flexibility. Governments can create enabling environments through financial incentives, research funding, and supportive market structures. Time-of-use tariffs, for instance, encourage consumers to adjust demand patterns in alignment with renewable availability. Capacity markets and ancillary service mechanisms reward flexible resources—such as storage systems or demand response—for providing stability and reliability to the grid. Public investment in transmission upgrades and interconnection infrastructure also plays a key role in integrating geographically diverse renewable resources, reducing regional imbalances and improving overall system efficiency.

Long-term planning and coordination are required to align storage development with renewable expansion. Policymakers and system operators must adopt integrated energy planning frameworks that consider multiple sectors—electricity, heating, transport, and industry—as interconnected components of one system. Electrification of end-use sectors increases the demand for flexible renewable generation, while advancements in vehicle-to-grid technologies enable electric vehicles to serve as distributed storage assets. Such cross-sectoral coordination ensures that variability is managed collectively rather than through isolated solutions.

Technological innovation continues to reshape the possibilities for managing renewable intermittency. Artificial intelligence and machine learning improve forecasting accuracy, allowing grid operators to predict renewable output more precisely. Predictive maintenance of renewable installations reduces downtime and maximizes generation potential. Advances in materials science and recycling enhance the sustainability of storage technologies, ensuring that circular principles extend to the components that underpin energy flexibility.

Addressing variability and storage challenges requires a balanced approach that combines technical innovation, market reform, and policy coherence. By investing in flexible grids, diversified storage technologies, and coordinated governance frameworks, societies can harness the full potential of renewable energy. These efforts ensure that clean energy systems operate reliably, efficiently, and equitably—laying the foundation for a circular energy economy capable of supporting long-term stability and growth.

Linking Renewable Energy to Resource Efficiency

The connection between renewable energy and resource efficiency is central to achieving a circular energy economy. Expanding renewable energy systems not only reduces emissions but also optimizes material use and minimizes waste throughout the entire energy life cycle. By aligning energy generation with efficient resource management, societies can ensure that the transition to clean power supports long-term sustainability without transferring environmental burdens to other sectors.

Renewable energy promotes resource efficiency by decoupling energy production from the extraction and depletion of finite resources. Conventional fossil fuel systems rely on constant mining, drilling, and transport, all of which demand substantial material and energy inputs. In contrast, renewable technologies harness naturally replenishing flows of energy that require minimal operational resources once installed. Solar, wind, hydro, and geothermal systems convert ambient energy into electricity without consuming the energy source itself. This inherent efficiency reduces pressure on ecosystems and lowers the material footprint associated with ongoing energy supply.

Lifecycle optimization is a key strategy for linking renewable energy expansion to resource conservation. It involves evaluating and improving every stage of a technology's existence—from raw material extraction and manufacturing to operation, maintenance, and end-of-life management. Circular design approaches focus on extending the lifespan of components, facilitating repair, and promoting reuse and recycling. For example, wind turbine blades and solar panel frames can be designed using modular construction, enabling parts to be replaced or upgraded without discarding entire units. Applying lifecycle analysis ensures that renewable infrastructure contributes to long-term sustainability rather than creating new waste streams.

Material recovery and recycling are essential to maintaining the resource efficiency of renewable systems. The growing demand for metals such as lithium, cobalt, and rare earth elements poses risks of resource depletion and environmental harm. A circular approach mitigates these risks by prioritizing secondary resource use and recycling critical materials. End-of-life collection systems for solar panels, wind turbines, and batteries enable the recovery of valuable components for reintroduction into new production cycles. Recycling not only conserves resources but also reduces the energy and emissions associated with mining and refining virgin materials.

Digital technologies enhance the synergy between renewable energy and resource efficiency by enabling precision management of energy and material flows. Smart sensors and data analytics track performance and predict maintenance needs, minimizing downtime and extending equipment life. Artificial intelligence optimizes energy production and consumption, ensuring that renewables operate at peak efficiency. Blockchain can trace material sourcing and recycling processes, enhancing transparency and accountability across supply chains. Together, these tools help close loops between energy use, material recovery, and resource management.

Integrating renewable energy into production systems also reduces material waste across industries. Electrifying industrial processes with renewables can improve efficiency and lower total resource inputs. For instance, green hydrogen produced from renewable electricity can replace fossil fuels in steel and chemical manufacturing, reducing both carbon emissions and waste by-products. In agriculture, renewable-powered irrigation and processing systems reduce water and fuel use while supporting circular nutrient cycles. Across sectors, coupling renewable energy with efficient technologies reinforces the principle of doing more with less.

Urban systems demonstrate how renewable energy expansion drives resource efficiency through integrated planning. Buildings designed with energy-efficient materials, solar roofs, and smart energy management systems consume fewer resources and operate more sustainably. Waste-to-energy systems convert municipal waste into renewable power, reducing landfill dependency while recovering energy from otherwise discarded materials. Electric public transport powered by renewables lowers fuel demand and enhances air quality, creating compounding benefits across urban systems.

Policy and regulation play a critical role in promoting lifecycle efficiency in renewable development. Governments can establish extended producer responsibility frameworks that require manufacturers to plan for product reuse and recycling. Standards for eco-design and resource recovery ensure that renewable technologies meet sustainability criteria throughout their lifecycles. Incentives for using recycled materials and for improving circular design stimulate innovation in resource-efficient technologies. These policy measures align market behavior with the goals of circularity, supporting an energy system that conserves rather than consumes resources.

The expansion of renewable energy, when aligned with lifecycle optimization and responsible resource management, transforms energy systems into circular, regenerative structures. It enables societies to meet growing energy demands while reducing waste, conserving materials, and respecting ecological boundaries. By viewing renewable energy not just as a source of power but as a catalyst for systemic efficiency, the circular energy economy advances both environmental integrity and long-term resilience.

Chapter 3: Energy Efficiency and Demand Optimization

Energy efficiency and demand optimization are central to achieving a circular energy economy. By reducing overall energy consumption and optimizing when and how energy is used, these strategies help decouple economic growth from resource use. This chapter examines efficiency as a core pillar of circularity, exploring the integration of smart technologies, behavioral change, and industrial innovation. It highlights how demand-side management, predictive analytics, and process optimization contribute to resource conservation and emission reduction. Together, these approaches demonstrate how energy efficiency transforms consumption patterns and supports the transition toward regenerative, low-carbon energy systems.

The Role of Efficiency in Circular Energy Systems

Efficiency is a foundational element of the circular energy economy, representing the bridge between resource conservation, emissions reduction, and system resilience. It is not merely about producing more with less but about rethinking how energy and materials flow through economies to eliminate waste and maximize value. In a circular context, efficiency functions as both a technical and systemic principle that underpins every aspect of sustainable energy management—from generation and distribution to consumption and recovery.

Energy efficiency traditionally refers to reducing the amount of energy required to deliver the same level of service. In circular systems, this concept expands to encompass material and process efficiency, recognizing that energy use and resource use are interconnected. Each stage of an energy system's lifecycle—extraction, production, transmission, and utilization—offers opportunities to minimize losses. Reducing these inefficiencies lowers not only energy demand but also associated emissions and material inputs. By optimizing conversion processes and system

29

performance, circular energy systems can significantly reduce their overall environmental footprint while maintaining or improving output.

At the generation stage, efficiency improvements increase the yield of renewable technologies and minimize the need for supplementary fossil generation. Advanced photovoltaic designs, high-efficiency wind turbines, and optimized hydropower systems convert a greater share of natural energy flows into usable electricity. In combined heat and power systems, waste heat from electricity production is captured and reused, enhancing total system efficiency. These integrated designs exemplify how efficiency enables circularity by ensuring that every available energy stream contributes to useful output rather than being discarded as waste.

Transmission and distribution systems also benefit from efficiency-oriented design. Smart grids, digital sensors, and automated control systems reduce transmission losses and enhance demand management. By adjusting energy flows in real time, these technologies align supply with consumption more precisely, minimizing wasteful overproduction and curtailment. Localized microgrids further improve efficiency by generating and consuming energy close to the point of use, cutting down on long-distance transmission losses. Together, these infrastructure-level efficiencies help create a flexible and responsive energy system capable of supporting higher shares of renewables.

End-use efficiency remains one of the most direct and impactful ways to achieve circularity. Buildings, transport, and industry account for the majority of global energy consumption, and each sector holds vast potential for reducing demand through technological and behavioral change. Retrofitting buildings with insulation, smart controls, and efficient lighting reduces heating and cooling loads. Electrification of transport, supported by renewable energy, eliminates combustion losses inherent in fossil fuel engines. In industry, process optimization, waste heat recovery, and advanced materials reduce both energy and raw material inputs. These improvements extend beyond economic savings, contributing to resource conservation and emissions mitigation across value chains.

Efficiency in circular systems also includes time and resource optimization through design thinking and lifecycle planning. Products and infrastructure designed for longevity, repairability, and modularity require fewer replacements and less energy-intensive manufacturing over time. Efficient use of materials in renewable technologies—such as substituting scarce minerals with abundant alternatives—reduces embedded energy and mitigates supply risks. Similarly, digitalization enables predictive maintenance and performance optimization, preventing failures and reducing the need for resource-intensive replacements. These measures reflect a shift from one-time efficiency gains to continuous, adaptive management of energy and materials.

Policy and governance frameworks play a crucial role in institutionalizing efficiency within circular systems. Energy efficiency standards, performance-based regulations, and incentive schemes encourage adoption of efficient technologies and practices. Carbon pricing and energy taxation can further internalize the environmental cost of inefficiency, making resource optimization a market imperative. Public awareness campaigns and energy labeling programs empower consumers to make efficient choices, reinforcing collective responsibility in achieving circular goals.

Efficiency serves as both the starting point and the ongoing driver of the circular energy transition. It minimizes inputs, reduces emissions, and extends the utility of every resource used. When applied holistically across production, infrastructure, and consumption, efficiency transforms linear systems into adaptive networks where waste is minimized, value is retained, and sustainability is embedded in every stage of the energy cycle.

Demand-Side Management and Behavioral Change

Demand-side management (DSM) is a cornerstone of the circular energy economy, emphasizing the role of consumers in achieving balance, efficiency, and flexibility across energy systems. Rather than focusing solely on expanding supply, DSM optimizes how, when, and where energy is used. By coordinating consumption patterns with renewable generation and incorporating behavioral change alongside smart technologies, DSM transforms consumers into active participants in maintaining stability and sustainability within circular energy systems.

At its core, DSM involves shaping demand to align with the availability of renewable energy. Traditional energy systems operate on the principle of meeting demand at all times, regardless of resource intensity or environmental cost. Circular energy systems invert this logic by encouraging consumption during periods of abundant renewable supply and minimizing it when generation is low. This coordination reduces reliance on fossil-based backup power and enhances the integration of variable renewables such as solar and wind. Demand flexibility, therefore, becomes a vital resource—complementing storage technologies and improving overall system efficiency.

Smart technologies play a pivotal role in enabling effective DSM. Advanced metering infrastructure, automated controls, and data analytics provide real-time visibility into energy consumption patterns, empowering users to make informed decisions. Smart grids communicate continuously with connected devices, adjusting power flows to maintain balance between supply and demand. For instance, household appliances, heating and cooling systems, and electric vehicle chargers can automatically operate during times of high renewable generation or low grid demand. This automation optimizes system performance while maintaining convenience for consumers.

Artificial intelligence (AI) enhances the sophistication of DSM by predicting consumption behavior and renewable output with greater accuracy. Machine learning algorithms analyze historical and environmental data to forecast demand trends and recommend optimal usage schedules. Utilities can use these insights to design dynamic pricing models, such as time-of-use tariffs, that incentivize users to shift consumption to periods of low demand or high renewable generation. This approach aligns economic signals with environmental objectives, reducing strain on infrastructure and supporting grid stability.

Behavioral change complements technological solutions by fostering long-term shifts in energy use habits. Awareness and education campaigns encourage consumers to understand the environmental impact of their energy choices and the benefits of adjusting consumption patterns. Simple actions—such as reducing peak-hour usage, adopting efficient appliances, or moderating thermostat settings—collectively produce significant system-level benefits. Over time, these behavioral adaptations cultivate a culture of shared responsibility, reinforcing the principles of efficiency and circularity.

Prosumers—individuals or organizations that both produce and consume energy—embody the intersection of behavioral change and technology-driven participation. With rooftop solar systems, home batteries, and electric vehicles, prosumers can manage their own energy production and consumption in coordination with grid conditions. They can store excess generation for personal use or sell it back to the grid through peer-to-peer trading platforms. This decentralized model not only empowers consumers but also strengthens energy resilience by diversifying generation sources and enhancing flexibility.

Community-level initiatives amplify the impact of DSM and behavioral change. Energy cooperatives and local microgrids enable collective management of renewable resources, where residents collaborate to optimize consumption and share benefits. Digital platforms allow for transparent tracking of usage and savings, promoting trust and participation. Such collaborative models integrate social innovation into circular energy systems, ensuring that technological advancements are accompanied by inclusive governance and equitable access.

Policy frameworks play a crucial role in supporting DSM and encouraging behavioral transformation. Governments and utilities can introduce regulatory mechanisms that reward participation in demand-response programs, promote real-time pricing, and ensure interoperability among smart technologies. Educational initiatives, financial incentives, and pilot projects accelerate adoption by demonstrating the practical and economic benefits of DSM. Public-sector leadership—through efficient public buildings, transportation networks, and infrastructure—sets examples that reinforce behavioral norms at scale.

The success of demand-side management lies in the synergy between individual behavior, collective participation, and technological intelligence. By aligning human decision-making with automated optimization systems, circular energy economies achieve a dynamic equilibrium between supply and demand. Consumers evolve into active contributors within interconnected networks, where every action—whether automated or deliberate—enhances resource efficiency, stability, and resilience across the energy system.

Industrial Efficiency and Waste Heat Recovery

Improving industrial efficiency and capturing waste heat are essential strategies for reducing energy demand, emissions, and resource use within the circular energy economy. Industries are among the largest consumers of energy, and a significant portion of that energy is lost as heat during production processes. By integrating advanced technologies for process optimization and waste heat utilization, industrial systems can close energy loops, converting losses into productive inputs while enhancing overall sustainability.

Industrial energy efficiency begins with optimizing production processes to minimize losses at every stage. Traditional manufacturing often involves high-temperature operations, mechanical work, and chemical transformations that consume vast amounts of energy. Inefficiencies arise through friction, heat dissipation, and outdated equipment design. Modern process integration techniques address these challenges by reconfiguring systems to maximize energy transfer and reuse. For example, heat exchangers recover thermal energy from exhaust gases or cooling fluids and redirect it to preheat raw materials or supply other process stages. This internal recycling of energy reduces the need for external inputs and lowers operational costs.

Waste heat recovery (WHR) technologies are central to industrial circularity. They capture energy that would otherwise be lost to the environment and convert it into usable forms of power or heat. The choice of technology depends on the temperature and composition of the waste stream. High-temperature waste heat, common in steel, cement, and glass industries, can be recovered using regenerative burners or combined heat and power (CHP) systems to generate electricity or steam. Medium- and low-temperature heat, found in sectors like food processing and textiles, can be harnessed through heat pumps, organic Rankine cycle (ORC) systems, or absorption chillers. These technologies allow industries to reuse waste energy internally or supply it to neighboring facilities or district energy networks.

The integration of WHR systems aligns with the broader principle of industrial symbiosis, where one facility's by-products become another's resources. Excess heat from industrial processes can provide heating for nearby residential or commercial buildings, while recovered steam can support other manufacturing operations. This exchange not only reduces total energy consumption but also strengthens regional resilience by creating interconnected, efficient production ecosystems. When combined with renewable energy sources, such systems further decarbonize industrial clusters and move them closer to circularity.

Digitalization enhances industrial efficiency by enabling precise monitoring and optimization of energy flows. Smart sensors and control systems collect real-time data on temperature, pressure, and energy use across processes. Advanced analytics and artificial intelligence identify inefficiencies, predict equipment failures, and recommend adjustments to maintain optimal performance. Predictive maintenance minimizes downtime and prevents unnecessary energy loss, while digital twins—virtual models of industrial systems—allow operators to simulate energy-saving scenarios and evaluate process modifications before implementation. These capabilities make efficiency gains continuous rather than one-time improvements.

Material efficiency complements energy efficiency within circular industrial systems. Many energy losses stem from material inefficiencies, such as excessive scrap production or poor thermal insulation. By improving process precision and reusing by-products, industries can reduce both energy and material waste. Closed-loop manufacturing, where production residues are recycled back into the process, conserves resources and eliminates disposal-related energy consumption. Advanced materials designed for high thermal resistance or lightweight performance also contribute to reducing energy intensity across industrial operations.

Policy and financial frameworks are instrumental in accelerating industrial efficiency and waste heat recovery. Governments can introduce energy performance standards, tax incentives, or grants for the adoption of WHR and process integration technologies. Carbon pricing further encourages industries to invest in efficiency improvements by internalizing the cost of emissions. Industrial energy audits and benchmarking programs provide valuable insights into efficiency opportunities and best practices. Public-private partnerships can also play a key role in developing shared infrastructure for waste heat utilization across industrial zones.

The future of industrial efficiency lies in the convergence of technology, design, and collaboration. As industries embrace circular models, waste heat will be increasingly recognized as a resource rather than a loss. Process integration, digital control, and energy recovery systems will operate in synergy, creating self-reinforcing loops of optimization. By capturing and reusing energy that once escaped into the environment, industries reduce emissions, lower costs, and contribute to a resilient, low-carbon economy built on the principles of circularity and regeneration.

Smart Grids and Digitalization for Efficiency

Smart grids and digital technologies are reshaping how energy systems operate, making them more adaptive, efficient, and responsive. These innovations enable real-time optimization of supply and demand, improve reliability, and facilitate the integration of renewable energy sources into existing networks. By embedding intelligence throughout the energy value chain, digitalization supports the circular energy economy's goal of reducing waste and maximizing system performance.

Smart grids enhance energy efficiency by allowing two-way communication between producers and consumers. Unlike traditional grids, which transmit electricity in a one-directional flow, smart grids use sensors, meters, and automated controls to gather and process data continuously. This real-time monitoring enables operators to detect inefficiencies, identify faults, and adjust operations instantly. Automation improves energy dispatch, reduces transmission losses, and supports the coordination of distributed renewable generation. These capabilities ensure that renewable power is used effectively and that grid stability is maintained under variable conditions.

Advanced metering infrastructure is a key component of smart grids, providing detailed insights into energy consumption patterns. Digital meters record usage in short intervals, allowing consumers and utilities to access accurate data on energy flows. This transparency empowers users to modify their behavior, shifting consumption to off-peak hours or periods of high renewable availability. For utilities, the data enables demand forecasting, targeted maintenance, and optimized load management. The result is a more efficient system where both supply and demand respond dynamically to real-time information.

Artificial intelligence and machine learning enhance the efficiency of digitalized grids by analyzing vast datasets to identify patterns and predict system behavior. Algorithms can forecast renewable generation based on weather data, anticipate equipment failures, and optimize energy dispatch. Predictive analytics also enables proactive maintenance, extending the lifespan of infrastructure and preventing energy losses associated with unplanned outages. These tools transform the grid into a self-learning system capable of continuous improvement and adaptation.

Energy storage systems benefit significantly from digital integration. Smart control systems manage when to charge or discharge storage units based on grid conditions and market signals. This coordination allows renewable energy to be stored during periods of excess generation and released when demand rises. Digitalization ensures that storage assets operate efficiently, providing frequency regulation, peak shaving, and backup power. By combining real-time data and intelligent control, smart grids make energy storage a central tool for balancing supply and demand.

Digitalization also facilitates sector coupling, linking electricity systems with heating, cooling, transport, and industry. Smart energy management platforms coordinate multiple energy carriers to improve overall system efficiency. For example, waste heat from industrial processes can be recovered and redirected into district heating networks, while excess renewable electricity can power electric vehicles or produce green hydrogen. These interconnections strengthen circularity by ensuring that no energy stream is wasted and that resources are used to their full potential.

Cyber-physical systems integrate digital technologies with physical infrastructure, creating a unified network of sensors, controllers, and actuators. These systems enable decentralized control, allowing local microgrids to operate autonomously or in coordination with the main grid. Microgrids powered by renewables and managed by digital systems can maintain energy supply during disruptions, contributing to resilience and local energy independence. Decentralized networks also promote consumer participation by enabling communities to generate, store, and share energy efficiently.

Policy and regulatory frameworks play a crucial role in advancing digitalization for efficiency. Governments can support investment in smart grid infrastructure, ensure data security, and establish standards for interoperability among devices and systems. Encouraging open data exchange between utilities and consumers fosters innovation and enhances transparency. Incentive programs for digital upgrades and research in artificial intelligence accelerate the adoption of intelligent energy management solutions.

Digitalization transforms the relationship between energy systems and users by enabling real-time optimization and greater interaction. Smart grids create the foundation for efficient, flexible, and renewable-powered energy systems that operate in harmony with circular principles. Through data-driven coordination and technological innovation, digitalization ensures that energy is produced, distributed, and consumed with maximum precision and minimal waste.

Chapter 4: Energy Storage and Resource Recovery

Energy storage and resource recovery are pivotal to creating stable and regenerative circular energy systems. By bridging gaps between variable renewable generation and consistent demand, storage technologies enhance flexibility, resilience, and reliability. This chapter explores diverse storage pathways—including batteries, thermal, mechanical, and hydrogen systems—while examining their design, lifecycle management, and circular potential. It also considers how waste-to-energy conversion and material recovery contribute to closing resource loops. Together, these elements illustrate how storage and recovery form the operational backbone of circular energy systems, ensuring continuity, efficiency, and sustainable use of energy and materials.

Circular Approaches to Energy Storage

Energy storage systems are essential to balancing supply and demand in renewable-based energy systems, enabling flexibility and stability in grids dominated by intermittent sources. As storage technologies expand globally, integrating circular principles into their design, use, and recovery becomes vital to minimizing environmental impact and conserving resources. Circular approaches to energy storage emphasize lifecycle management, material recovery, and the reuse of components, ensuring that storage systems support sustainable and resilient energy transitions.

Circular design begins with the selection of materials and components that enable durability, repairability, and recyclability. Batteries and other storage devices contain valuable and finite materials such as lithium, cobalt, nickel, and rare earth elements. Designing systems for easy disassembly allows these materials to be recovered and reused at the end of the product's life, reducing dependence on mining and lowering environmental footprints. Modular construction, standardization of components, and the use of non-toxic or recyclable materials further support circularity by simplifying maintenance and extending product lifespans.

Lifecycle management involves optimizing the use of storage systems throughout their operational life to extract maximum value before they reach the recycling stage. Advanced monitoring technologies track performance, degradation rates, and operational conditions in real time. Data analytics and predictive algorithms identify opportunities for maintenance or reconfiguration to extend useful life. For instance, battery management systems can balance charge cycles across cells, preventing premature failure and ensuring consistent performance. These strategies align with the circular goal of keeping energy assets in use for as long as possible while maintaining efficiency and safety.

Battery recycling is a key component of circular storage systems. End-of-life batteries contain recoverable metals and materials that can be reprocessed for new manufacturing. Recycling processes such as pyrometallurgical, hydrometallurgical, and direct recycling methods extract lithium, cobalt, and nickel with increasing efficiency. Improvements in recycling technologies continue to reduce energy use and emissions associated with these processes. Establishing robust collection systems and standardized recycling practices ensures that valuable resources are recirculated back into production, reducing pressure on raw material supply chains and minimizing waste.

Second-life applications extend the utility of batteries that no longer meet the performance requirements for their original use but still retain sufficient capacity for less demanding applications. For example, electric vehicle batteries can be repurposed for stationary energy storage in buildings, microgrids, or renewable energy systems. These second-life uses defer recycling and provide cost-effective storage solutions for communities and industries. Integrating second-life batteries into local energy networks enhances flexibility and contributes to circularity by maintaining the value of existing materials and manufacturing inputs.

Alternative storage technologies also present opportunities for circular innovation. Flow batteries, compressed air energy storage, and thermal storage systems can be designed with recyclable materials and modular structures that simplify maintenance and component replacement. Hydrogen storage, for instance, can be developed using renewable-powered electrolysis, producing a clean and recyclable energy carrier. Incorporating circular principles from the early stages of technology development ensures that emerging storage solutions avoid the waste and inefficiencies associated with linear models.

Digitalization supports circular energy storage by enabling traceability, performance tracking, and resource management. Blockchain and digital product passports can record the origin, composition, and lifecycle history of storage systems, facilitating recycling and repurposing. Real-time data analytics improve system efficiency and inform decisions on maintenance, replacement, or reuse. These tools create feedback loops that enhance resource efficiency across the entire value chain.

Policy measures are essential for scaling circular energy storage. Governments can promote extended producer responsibility, requiring manufacturers to manage end-of-life recovery and recycling. Standards for eco-design, labeling, and material recovery ensure consistency and transparency across markets. Financial incentives for recycling infrastructure, second-life projects, and research in circular materials accelerate progress. Collaborative partnerships between industry, academia, and governments can foster innovation and establish best practices for sustainable storage ecosystems.

Circular approaches to energy storage create systems that are not only functional and efficient but also regenerative. By prioritizing design for longevity, reuse, and recovery, storage technologies become integral to a sustainable energy future. They transform energy storage from a temporary solution into a continuous cycle of resource optimization, supporting the broader goals of resilience, decarbonization, and circularity in global energy systems.

Material Circularity in Battery Supply Chains

Battery supply chains are at the core of the global energy transition, powering technologies from electric vehicles to renewable energy storage systems. However, their rapid expansion has intensified demand for critical minerals such as lithium, cobalt, nickel, and manganese, raising environmental and social concerns related to mining, processing, and waste. Material circularity in battery supply chains addresses these challenges by promoting sustainable sourcing, reuse, and recycling. Through closed-loop systems and responsible material management, circular approaches reduce resource dependency, minimize ecological harm, and enhance long-term resilience in energy storage ecosystems.

Sustainable sourcing forms the foundation of circular battery supply chains. Mining operations for critical minerals often occur in regions with fragile ecosystems and complex social conditions. Circular strategies emphasize responsible extraction practices that meet environmental and labor standards, reduce water and land impacts, and prioritize transparency across supply networks. Certification schemes, such as the Initiative for Responsible Mining Assurance and the Global Battery Alliance's Battery Passport, help trace materials from mine to market, ensuring compliance with ethical and environmental benchmarks. Additionally, diversifying sources— including recycling and secondary raw materials—reduces reliance on high-risk or geopolitically sensitive regions.

Designing batteries with circularity in mind enhances resource recovery and minimizes material waste. Manufacturers increasingly adopt eco-design principles that prioritize recyclability, standardization, and modularity. Simplified cell architecture and the use of non-hazardous binders or solvents make batteries easier to disassemble and process at the end of their lifecycle. Design improvements that allow for easier separation of components such as cathodes, anodes, and electrolytes facilitate more efficient recycling and reduce the energy required for material recovery. Standardized formats across battery types can also streamline collection and recycling operations, enabling economies of scale.

Reuse and remanufacturing extend the functional life of battery components before recycling becomes necessary. Cells or modules that fall below the performance requirements for electric vehicles can be tested, reconfigured, and redeployed in less demanding applications, such as stationary storage or backup power systems. This approach delays the need for new mineral extraction and maximizes the value extracted from existing materials. Manufacturers and utilities increasingly establish partnerships for second-life battery projects, creating a secondary market that supports both economic and environmental goals.

Recycling remains a critical pillar of material circularity in battery supply chains. Advanced recycling technologies enable the recovery of valuable metals from spent batteries, reducing the need for new mining and minimizing waste. Hydrometallurgical and direct recycling processes achieve higher recovery rates while consuming less energy and generating fewer emissions compared to traditional pyrometallurgical methods. These techniques allow materials such as lithium, cobalt, and nickel to be reintroduced into new battery production, closing the material loop. As recycling infrastructure expands, the proportion of secondary raw materials in battery manufacturing is expected to increase, strengthening the resilience of supply chains against resource scarcity and price volatility.

Digitalization enhances traceability and efficiency throughout the circular battery value chain. Tools such as blockchain-based tracking systems record each material's origin, ownership, and processing history, providing transparency and enabling compliance with sustainability standards. Digital product passports store detailed information on battery composition, manufacturing date, and recycling pathways, supporting efficient collection and recovery. These technologies also improve inventory management for manufacturers and recyclers, ensuring that valuable materials are recovered promptly and reused effectively.

Policy frameworks are vital to advancing material circularity in battery supply chains. Extended producer responsibility regulations require manufacturers to take accountability for the end-of-life management of their products. Incentives for recycling infrastructure, research in substitution materials, and the use of recycled content encourage market participation. International cooperation and harmonized standards are essential for managing transboundary material flows and preventing waste export to regions with weaker environmental safeguards.

Material circularity in battery supply chains transforms how critical minerals are sourced, used, and recovered. By integrating sustainable extraction, design for recyclability, second-life applications, and advanced recycling technologies, circular systems preserve valuable resources and reduce environmental pressures. These practices not only strengthen energy security but also align the storage sector with broader goals of sustainability, transparency, and responsible growth within the circular energy economy.

Thermal, Mechanical, and Hydrogen Storage Pathways

A diverse portfolio of energy storage technologies is essential to balance renewable energy supply and demand across different time scales and applications. While electrochemical batteries dominate short-term storage, thermal, mechanical, and hydrogen-based systems play critical roles in providing medium- to long-term flexibility. Each pathway offers distinct advantages in efficiency, scalability, and integration potential, contributing to the overall stability and circularity of renewable energy systems.

Thermal energy storage (TES) captures heat or cold for later use, supporting both electricity and heating networks. TES systems store excess energy as heat in materials such as molten salts, phase-change materials, or solid media like concrete or rock. When electricity demand rises or renewable output declines, the stored heat can be converted back into electricity through turbines or used directly for industrial processes and district heating. These systems are particularly valuable for integrating solar thermal and waste heat recovery applications. Concentrated solar power plants often employ molten salt storage to supply electricity during nighttime or cloudy periods, effectively decoupling generation from sunlight availability. TES can also enhance building efficiency by storing thermal energy from renewable sources for heating or cooling, reducing reliance on fossil-based systems.

Mechanical storage technologies convert energy into mechanical motion or potential energy for later reconversion into electricity. The most established method, pumped hydro storage (PHS), uses gravitational potential energy by pumping water to an elevated reservoir during periods of low demand and releasing it through turbines when demand increases. PHS provides large-scale, long-duration storage with high round-trip efficiency and remains the backbone of many national grid balancing strategies. Its main limitation lies in geographic requirements, prompting exploration of new approaches such as underground or modular systems that reduce environmental impact.

Compressed air energy storage (CAES) and flywheels represent other key mechanical pathways. CAES systems compress air into underground caverns or storage tanks during surplus generation and release it through turbines to generate electricity during peak demand. Modern adiabatic CAES systems recover and reuse the heat produced during compression, improving efficiency and aligning with circular energy principles. Flywheels, on the other hand, store energy in the rotational motion of a high-speed rotor. Although suited for shorter durations, they provide rapid response and high cycling capability, making them ideal for stabilizing grids with variable renewable inputs. The durability and recyclability of mechanical storage materials also contribute to circularity, as many components can be repurposed or remanufactured with minimal degradation.

Hydrogen storage offers one of the most flexible and far-reaching pathways for renewable integration. When renewable energy generation exceeds demand, excess electricity can be used to produce hydrogen through electrolysis. The hydrogen can then be stored in tanks, underground caverns, or pipelines and later reconverted into electricity using fuel cells or combustion turbines.

Unlike batteries, hydrogen enables large-scale, long-duration energy storage suitable for seasonal balancing. It also supports sector coupling by serving as a feedstock for industry, transport, and heating. For instance, green hydrogen produced from renewables can replace fossil fuels in steel manufacturing or serve as a fuel for heavy transport and shipping. By linking electricity with multiple sectors, hydrogen storage strengthens overall system efficiency and resilience.

Integrating these diverse storage technologies creates a multi-layered energy system capable of handling variability across time frames. Short-term storage such as batteries and flywheels address rapid fluctuations, while medium- and long-term solutions like TES, CAES, and hydrogen provide sustained balancing capacity. Hybrid systems that combine different storage types offer additional flexibility; for example, using batteries for quick response and hydrogen or thermal storage for extended discharge periods. These configurations ensure reliability while maximizing renewable utilization and minimizing curtailment.

Digitalization enhances the performance and coordination of storage systems. Advanced control algorithms and predictive analytics optimize charging and discharging cycles, coordinate storage assets, and forecast renewable output and demand patterns. Smart grids and energy management platforms integrate diverse storage systems into cohesive networks, ensuring that each technology operates within its optimal range. This digital coordination aligns with circular energy principles by minimizing losses and extending equipment lifespan through intelligent operation.

Policy and investment frameworks are crucial for scaling non-battery storage pathways. Supportive regulations, research funding, and market mechanisms that value flexibility services encourage innovation and deployment. Standardizing safety and performance metrics for hydrogen and thermal systems builds market confidence, while incentives for hybrid projects promote integrated solutions. International collaboration on technology standards and infrastructure planning helps accelerate adoption and ensure interoperability across borders.

Thermal, mechanical, and hydrogen storage pathways collectively enhance the resilience and adaptability of renewable energy systems. Their complementary characteristics enable reliable power supply, efficient resource use, and systemic balance. By embedding circular principles through resource recovery, lifecycle design, and cross-sector integration, these storage technologies form an indispensable part of the transition toward a sustainable, renewable-based energy future.

Waste-to-Energy and Resource Recovery Integration

Waste-to-energy (WtE) and resource recovery systems play an important role in advancing the circular energy economy by converting residual waste streams into usable energy and materials. These systems bridge the gap between waste management and renewable energy generation, reducing landfill dependency while contributing to energy security and resource efficiency. By integrating WtE technologies into circular frameworks, societies can transform waste from an environmental burden into a valuable resource that complements renewable systems and strengthens overall sustainability.

WtE technologies convert non-recyclable waste materials into electricity, heat, or fuels through processes such as combustion, gasification, pyrolysis, and anaerobic digestion. Each method recovers the embedded energy content of waste while minimizing disposal volumes. Conventional incineration with energy recovery remains the most widely deployed approach, generating heat and electricity from municipal solid waste. Modern facilities employ advanced emission control systems and energy-efficient designs to meet environmental standards while maximizing recovery. Gasification and pyrolysis offer cleaner alternatives by converting waste into synthetic gas or bio-oil, which can be refined into fuels or used for power generation. These technologies provide flexible options for integrating waste management with renewable energy production, reducing reliance on fossil fuels.

Anaerobic digestion exemplifies a circular process by transforming organic waste—such as food residues, agricultural by-products, and sewage sludge—into biogas and digestate. The biogas can be upgraded into biomethane for injection into natural gas grids or used to generate electricity and heat, while the digestate serves as a nutrient-rich fertilizer. This closed-loop approach supports agricultural sustainability, reduces methane emissions from landfills, and provides renewable energy that complements intermittent solar and wind resources. As urban populations grow, decentralized anaerobic digestion systems offer localized solutions for both waste treatment and energy supply.

Integrating WtE within broader renewable systems enhances energy system flexibility and reliability. While renewables such as solar and wind are variable, WtE plants provide continuous, dispatchable power. This stable output supports grid balancing and ensures a consistent supply during periods of low renewable generation. Additionally, integrating WtE with district heating and cooling networks maximizes energy efficiency by utilizing recovered heat for residential and industrial use. Co-location of WtE facilities with industrial parks allows for the direct use of heat and power in manufacturing, fostering industrial symbiosis and minimizing transmission losses.

Resource recovery is integral to circular WtE systems. Beyond energy production, advanced sorting and recycling technologies extract valuable materials—such as metals, glass, and plastics—from waste streams before energy conversion. Bottom ash from incineration can be processed to recover metals and minerals for construction materials, further reducing landfill disposal. These processes create multi-output recovery systems where both materials and energy are reclaimed, contributing to circularity and minimizing environmental impacts. Integrating digital monitoring and automated sorting improves recovery rates, ensuring that only non-recyclable fractions proceed to energy conversion.

Circularity in WtE extends to emissions management and carbon recovery. Modern plants capture carbon dioxide from flue gases for use in industrial applications or for storage, creating pathways toward carbon-neutral or carbon-negative energy. When combined with bio-based waste feedstocks, WtE systems can achieve net-negative emissions through bioenergy with carbon capture and storage (BECCS). This integration aligns with broader decarbonization strategies by turning waste streams into tools for carbon mitigation rather than sources of pollution.

Policy frameworks are central to promoting WtE and resource recovery integration within circular economies. Governments can support these systems through regulations that prioritize energy recovery after reuse and recycling, financial incentives for low-emission technologies, and targets for landfill diversion. Extended producer responsibility schemes encourage product designs that facilitate recycling and reduce residual waste. Public-private partnerships and municipal programs can mobilize investment in modern WtE infrastructure, ensuring scalability and long-term operation aligned with environmental objectives.

Technological innovation continues to improve the efficiency and sustainability of WtE systems. Advances in plasma gasification, catalytic conversion, and biological treatment enhance energy yields and minimize by-products. Integration with digital platforms enables real-time monitoring of plant performance and emissions, ensuring transparency and continuous optimization. As part of urban infrastructure, smart WtE facilities can dynamically adjust operation based on waste generation patterns and energy demand.

The synergy between waste-to-energy systems and renewable energy enhances both energy resilience and resource efficiency. By converting unavoidable waste into clean energy and valuable materials, WtE serves as a critical component of circular systems that minimize environmental impact while maximizing resource recovery. When integrated thoughtfully with recycling, renewable generation, and carbon management strategies, these technologies close loops within the energy and material cycles, supporting the broader goal of sustainable and regenerative growth.

Chapter 5: Circular Design in Energy Infrastructure

Circular design in energy infrastructure focuses on creating systems that are durable, adaptable, and regenerative throughout their lifecycles. By applying circular economy principles to the design of power plants, grids, and energy storage systems, this approach reduces material waste, enhances resource efficiency, and extends asset longevity. This chapter examines how modularity, flexibility, and recyclability are integrated into infrastructure planning and engineering. It explores strategies for retrofitting existing assets, optimizing material flows, and designing for disassembly and reuse. Through circular design, energy infrastructure becomes a foundation for long-term sustainability, resilience, and continuous innovation.

Designing Infrastructure for Longevity and Adaptability

Designing energy infrastructure for longevity and adaptability is a fundamental principle of the circular energy economy. Traditional infrastructure has often been built for fixed functions and limited operational lifespans, leading to premature obsolescence, high maintenance costs, and significant environmental impacts. In contrast, circular design emphasizes flexibility, modularity, and durability—ensuring that systems can evolve with technological, environmental, and social changes while minimizing the need for new material inputs. This approach extends asset life, reduces waste, and supports the efficient use of resources across the energy value chain.

Longevity in infrastructure begins with material selection and structural integrity. Using durable, high-quality materials ensures that assets remain operational for decades with minimal degradation. Design choices that facilitate easy inspection, maintenance, and component replacement enhance long-term performance and reduce the frequency of full system overhauls. For example, selecting corrosion-resistant materials in pipelines, transmission lines, and storage systems extends operational life and lowers lifecycle costs. Adopting standardized components allows infrastructure to remain compatible with future upgrades, avoiding the inefficiencies associated with one-time, non-reusable installations.

Modular design is central to adaptability and circularity. Modular systems are built from interchangeable units that can be replaced, upgraded, or reconfigured without dismantling entire structures. This flexibility allows infrastructure to adapt to changing energy demands, technologies, and policies. In renewable energy systems, modular solar panels, battery units, and wind turbine components can be added or replaced as efficiency improves, keeping the overall system current and functional. In power grids, modular substations and digital control systems allow utilities to integrate new technologies without extensive reconstruction. Modular design also simplifies repair and recycling processes, as components can be easily separated for maintenance or material recovery.

Adaptability ensures that energy infrastructure can evolve alongside technological advancements and market transformations. Designing systems that can accommodate new functions or operate in multiple configurations enhances their long-term relevance. For instance, power plants initially designed for fossil fuels can be retrofitted to operate with renewable gases or hydrogen. Transmission networks can be reconfigured to accommodate distributed generation and microgrids. This capacity for transformation prevents assets from becoming stranded and aligns infrastructure development with the principles of resource efficiency and long-term resilience.

Digitalization supports longevity and adaptability by providing data-driven insights into infrastructure performance. Smart monitoring systems use sensors and analytics to detect inefficiencies, predict maintenance needs, and identify opportunities for optimization. Predictive maintenance minimizes unplanned downtime and extends the useful life of equipment by addressing wear before it leads to failure. Digital twins—virtual replicas of physical assets—allow operators to simulate performance under different scenarios and assess the impacts of potential upgrades. This proactive approach reduces resource waste and ensures that maintenance activities are targeted and efficient.

Designing for disassembly and recyclability complements modularity and longevity. When infrastructure reaches the end of its service life, components designed for easy separation and recovery can be reused or recycled, reducing environmental footprints. For example, wind turbine blades, solar panels, and energy storage systems can be designed with recyclable materials and minimal adhesives to facilitate recovery. Incorporating cradle-to-cradle principles during the design phase ensures that materials remain in circulation rather than becoming waste. This design philosophy transforms infrastructure from a linear consumption model into a regenerative system.

Policy and investment frameworks play a crucial role in promoting infrastructure longevity and adaptability. Governments can encourage circular design through procurement standards that prioritize lifecycle value over upfront cost, tax incentives for modular construction, and regulations requiring recyclability in critical components. Long-term planning that integrates flexibility into national energy strategies ensures that public investments remain viable as technologies and market conditions evolve. Financial instruments such as green bonds and sustainability-linked loans can support infrastructure projects that meet durability and adaptability criteria.

Designing infrastructure for longevity and adaptability embodies the shift from short-term construction to long-term stewardship of assets. Through modular design, flexible functionality, and digital innovation, energy systems can evolve sustainably without continuous replacement or expansion. This approach conserves materials, reduces emissions, and creates infrastructure that remains resilient and efficient throughout its lifecycle, aligning built environments with the regenerative principles of the circular energy economy.

Urban and Industrial Symbiosis

Urban and industrial symbiosis represents a practical expression of circular economy principles, focusing on collaboration between different sectors to optimize resource use and minimize waste. It involves creating shared infrastructure and systems that enable the exchange of energy, materials, water, and information between industries and urban areas. By linking producers and consumers through symbiotic networks, these models transform waste from one process into valuable inputs for another, enhancing efficiency, reducing emissions, and supporting regional sustainability.

Industrial symbiosis emerged from the idea that industrial systems could function like natural ecosystems, where outputs and by-products circulate continuously within a closed loop. The concept extends beyond individual companies to entire industrial parks or regions. Factories, utilities, and service providers collaborate to share resources and infrastructure such as heat networks, water recycling systems, and waste treatment facilities. This interconnected approach reduces resource demand and operational costs while fostering innovation through collective problem-solving. Successful examples demonstrate that industrial symbiosis can significantly cut emissions, reduce waste generation, and strengthen local economies by creating new business opportunities.

In urban contexts, symbiosis connects cities and industries through shared resource flows and integrated planning. Urban areas generate large quantities of organic waste, wastewater, and heat, all of which can be recovered and repurposed. Wastewater treatment plants, for instance, can supply reclaimed water for industrial processes or irrigation, while organic waste can be processed into biogas for electricity and heat generation. Waste heat from industrial operations can be distributed through district heating networks to supply residential and commercial buildings. These systems transform cities into active participants in circular resource management, aligning urban development with industrial sustainability.

Shared infrastructure forms the backbone of urban and industrial symbiosis. Co-located industries can benefit from joint energy production, waste treatment, and logistics systems, reducing duplication and improving resource efficiency. Combined heat and power (CHP) plants provide an example of this integration, producing electricity and recovering waste heat for use across multiple facilities. Similarly, centralized water recycling systems treat and redistribute process water among industrial users, lowering freshwater demand. Shared logistics platforms reduce transportation emissions by coordinating freight movement and optimizing supply chains. This level of integration creates economies of scale and environmental benefits that individual companies could not achieve independently.

Digitalization enhances symbiosis by enabling precise monitoring and coordination of resource exchanges. Smart metering, sensors, and data platforms allow industries and municipalities to track flows of energy, materials, and waste in real time. Artificial intelligence and data analytics identify inefficiencies, forecast demand, and optimize resource allocation across participants. Digital platforms can match waste producers with potential users, facilitating transactions and ensuring that resources are directed to their highest-value applications. This digital connectivity transforms symbiosis from static networks into dynamic, adaptive systems that continuously evolve and improve performance.

Policy frameworks and governance structures are essential to fostering urban and industrial symbiosis. Local and regional authorities play a coordinating role by facilitating partnerships, establishing regulatory incentives, and providing shared infrastructure. Zoning policies that cluster complementary industries within designated eco-industrial parks encourage collaboration. Financial mechanisms such as subsidies for resource-sharing projects or tax reductions for using recovered materials can accelerate participation. Public-private partnerships often provide the investment and operational expertise necessary to establish and maintain symbiotic systems at scale.

Social and economic collaboration are also key elements of symbiosis. Building trust and long-term relationships among stakeholders encourages information exchange and joint innovation. Knowledge-sharing networks and research collaborations help identify new symbiotic opportunities and spread best practices. The inclusion of local communities in planning ensures that projects generate social as well as environmental benefits, such as job creation, cleaner air, and improved urban amenities.

Urban and industrial symbiosis contributes to the resilience of cities and industries by diversifying resource sources and reducing dependency on external inputs. By transforming waste into a resource and linking production with consumption through shared infrastructure, symbiotic systems embody the core principles of circularity. They create integrated, efficient, and adaptive networks that enhance sustainability while supporting economic vitality and social well-being.

Retrofitting Existing Energy Systems

Retrofitting existing energy systems is a critical strategy for achieving a circular and low-carbon future without discarding valuable infrastructure. Many of today's energy assets—power plants, grids, pipelines, and industrial facilities—were built for a linear, fossil-based model that prioritized extraction and throughput rather than efficiency and regeneration. Transforming these aging systems through targeted retrofits allows them to remain functional while aligning with circular principles of resource efficiency, adaptability, and longevity. This approach minimizes material waste, extends asset life, and accelerates the transition toward renewable and decentralized energy systems.

Retrofitting begins with identifying the most suitable assets for transformation. Many existing facilities can be upgraded to improve efficiency, reduce emissions, and integrate renewable energy sources. Power plants originally designed for coal or natural gas, for example, can be converted to run on biomass, biogas, or hydrogen, significantly reducing their carbon intensity. Turbine and boiler modifications, fuel-flexible burners, and carbon capture systems enable these plants to continue operating within decarbonization frameworks. Similarly, retrofitting industrial processes with advanced heat recovery and energy management systems can achieve substantial energy savings while reducing operational costs.

One of the most impactful retrofit opportunities lies in modernizing electricity grids. Traditional grids were built for one-way power flows from centralized generation to consumers. The rise of distributed renewables—such as rooftop solar, wind farms, and community microgrids—requires a bidirectional, intelligent network capable of managing dynamic energy exchanges. Upgrading transmission lines, substations, and control systems with smart grid technologies improves flexibility, reliability, and efficiency. Advanced sensors, automated switches, and digital control platforms enable real-time management of loads and distributed generation, allowing legacy grids to accommodate high shares of renewables without instability.

Retrofitting also applies to storage and balancing infrastructure. Many older hydroelectric plants can be enhanced with reversible turbines and digital controls to function as pumped storage systems, providing large-scale flexibility for renewable integration. Retrofitting existing gas storage facilities for hydrogen or biomethane storage creates additional value by repurposing established assets rather than constructing new ones. These interventions reduce the material and financial costs of new infrastructure while supporting the transition to diversified, low-carbon energy carriers.

District heating and cooling networks offer further retrofit potential. Older systems that rely on fossil-based heat sources can be connected to renewable and recovered energy streams, such as geothermal energy, industrial waste heat, or waste-to-energy plants. Integrating thermal storage and smart control systems enhances efficiency and responsiveness. In urban settings, combining retrofitted district systems with building energy upgrades—such as improved insulation, efficient heat pumps, and rooftop solar thermal collectors—creates synergies that reduce energy demand and emissions simultaneously.

Retrofitting also addresses the circular use of materials and equipment. Many existing infrastructure components contain valuable metals, composites, and mechanical systems that can be refurbished, reused, or remanufactured. Instead of full replacement, components such as transformers, turbines, and pipelines can undergo refurbishment programs that restore functionality with minimal resource input. This approach conserves materials and reduces the embodied energy of new construction. In renewable systems, repowering older wind farms by replacing outdated turbines with more efficient models maximizes land and grid use while extending project lifetimes.

Digitalization plays a central role in optimizing retrofit projects. Data-driven diagnostics and predictive analytics identify inefficiencies and prioritize interventions where they yield the greatest benefits. Digital twins enable operators to simulate retrofit scenarios, evaluate performance outcomes, and plan upgrades with minimal disruption. Real-time monitoring systems track progress and verify improvements in energy efficiency, emissions, and operational stability. Integrating digital solutions into retrofitted systems ensures that efficiency gains are sustained through continuous feedback and adaptive management.

Policy frameworks and investment strategies are key to scaling retrofits. Governments can create supportive environments by offering tax incentives, grants, and low-interest loans for modernization projects that improve circularity and reduce emissions. Regulations can require lifecycle assessments for large infrastructure projects, ensuring that retrofit options are considered before new construction. Public-private partnerships can mobilize expertise and capital to implement large-scale retrofits in critical sectors, such as power generation, transport, and industry.

Retrofitting aging energy systems aligns with both economic and environmental objectives. It enables countries to leverage existing assets while accelerating progress toward renewable integration and carbon neutrality. By embedding circular principles—efficiency, adaptability, and resource recovery—into the transformation of legacy infrastructure, retrofitting turns the challenges of aging systems into opportunities for innovation. The result is an adaptive, future-ready energy network that supports sustainability while preserving the value of past investments.

Life-Cycle Assessment and Material Efficiency

Life-cycle assessment (LCA) and material efficiency are essential tools for advancing circularity in energy infrastructure. They provide a framework for evaluating environmental performance across every stage of an asset's life—from raw material extraction and manufacturing to operation, maintenance, and end-of-life management. By identifying where resources are consumed and emissions generated, these tools guide decision-makers in optimizing design, extending asset life, and minimizing waste. When applied systematically, LCA and material efficiency help ensure that infrastructure development supports the broader goals of sustainability, resilience, and long-term resource conservation.

LCA examines the complete environmental footprint of a product or system, accounting for all inputs and outputs associated with its lifecycle. This includes energy use, material consumption, emissions, and waste at each stage of production, operation, and disposal. The analysis often considers multiple impact categories, such as carbon footprint, water use, toxicity, and land disturbance. By quantifying these impacts, LCA allows comparisons between different design options, materials, or technologies. For example, an LCA of a power plant may reveal that a slightly more expensive material with higher durability results in lower total emissions over the facility's lifetime. This holistic perspective ensures that efficiency and sustainability are addressed beyond the operational phase alone.

In the context of the circular energy economy, LCA plays a crucial role in preventing problem shifting—where reducing one type of environmental impact inadvertently increases another. For instance, substituting fossil fuels with renewable technologies reduces emissions but may increase mineral extraction. Conducting LCAs helps identify such trade-offs, allowing policymakers and engineers to design solutions that deliver net-positive outcomes. Moreover, integrating LCA into early project planning supports more informed investment decisions and aligns infrastructure development with national and corporate sustainability goals.

Material efficiency complements LCA by focusing on how materials are selected, used, and managed throughout their life cycles. Improving material efficiency means achieving the same or better functionality with fewer resources and less waste. This can be accomplished through lightweight design, modular construction, reuse of existing components, and increased recycling rates. In infrastructure projects, enhancing material efficiency reduces embodied energy—the total energy required to produce and transport materials—thus lowering overall carbon emissions. For renewable energy systems, material efficiency is particularly relevant, as technologies such as wind turbines, solar panels, and batteries rely on critical minerals with limited supply.

Tools and metrics developed for assessing material efficiency provide quantifiable insights into resource use. Indicators such as material intensity (the amount of material used per unit of output), recycling rates, and circularity indices measure how effectively resources are utilized. These metrics help identify opportunities for improvement, such as replacing scarce materials with abundant alternatives or extending the lifespan of structural components. When combined with LCA, they provide a comprehensive understanding of both the environmental and resource-related performance of infrastructure systems.

Digitalization enhances the accuracy and accessibility of LCA and material efficiency assessments. Advanced software platforms integrate real-time data from design, construction, and operation phases, allowing continuous monitoring of environmental performance. Digital twins can model infrastructure lifecycles, simulate scenarios, and evaluate the effects of design changes on energy and material use. Blockchain technology enables traceability of materials across supply chains, ensuring that sourcing and recycling practices align with circular principles. These digital tools make it possible to embed lifecycle thinking into everyday decision-making, supporting adaptive management and transparent reporting.

Policy frameworks and industry standards are instrumental in mainstreaming LCA and material efficiency. Governments can require lifecycle assessments as part of environmental permitting, procurement, and investment evaluation. Green building and infrastructure certification systems—such as LEED, BREEAM, and Envision—incorporate LCA-based criteria, rewarding projects that minimize embodied carbon and maximize resource reuse. Public agencies can lead by example, integrating material efficiency targets into infrastructure plans and funding mechanisms. Collaboration between policymakers, industry, and research institutions further supports the development of standardized methodologies and databases that improve consistency across sectors.

Embedding LCA and material efficiency into energy infrastructure planning ensures that sustainability goals extend beyond operational performance to encompass the full lifecycle of assets. This approach supports the design of systems that are durable, resource-conscious, and adaptable to future needs. By quantifying impacts, promoting informed choices, and integrating continuous improvement, LCA and material efficiency provide the analytical foundation for achieving circularity in the energy sector. Through their combined application, energy infrastructure becomes not only more efficient in operation but also more responsible in its creation, use, and eventual transformation.

Chapter 6: Circular Business Models and Financing Mechanisms

Circular business models and financing mechanisms redefine how value is created, delivered, and sustained in the energy sector. Moving beyond conventional ownership and consumption models, circular approaches emphasize shared use, service-based delivery, and lifecycle responsibility. This chapter explores how energy-as-a-service models, leasing structures, and product stewardship support long-term sustainability. It also examines innovative financing instruments—such as green bonds, blended finance, and impact investment—that enable the scaling of circular energy initiatives. Together, these elements illustrate how circular business and financial systems align profitability with resource regeneration, driving the transition toward a resilient, low-carbon energy economy.

Shifting from Ownership to Service-Based Models

The transition from ownership to service-based business models marks a significant evolution in the energy sector, reflecting the broader principles of the circular economy. Instead of focusing on the sale of physical assets or units of energy, these models prioritize delivering energy services, performance, and outcomes. By redefining value creation around access, efficiency, and longevity rather than ownership, service-based models promote resource optimization, reduce waste, and align financial incentives with sustainability goals.

Energy-as-a-service (EaaS) is one of the most prominent examples of this transformation. Under this model, customers pay for energy services—such as lighting, heating, cooling, or power availability—rather than for the energy itself or the equipment used to generate it. The provider retains ownership of the infrastructure, taking responsibility for operation, maintenance, and performance optimization. This structure encourages providers to design and manage systems that are energy-efficient, durable, and adaptable, since their revenue depends on service quality and cost-effectiveness rather than volume of consumption.

EaaS models shift the economic logic of the energy sector from consumption-based growth to efficiency-driven performance. Traditional energy markets reward higher sales volumes, often leading to increased emissions and resource depletion. In contrast, service-based systems incentivize the reduction of waste and the use of renewable sources. Providers benefit from minimizing operational costs through efficient technologies, smart energy management, and integration of renewable energy, while customers enjoy predictable costs and access to clean, reliable energy without the burden of ownership or technical expertise.

These models also enable broader participation in the energy transition. Businesses, municipalities, and households that may lack the capital or expertise to invest in renewable systems can access clean energy through service agreements. For example, solar-as-a-service allows users to benefit from solar power without purchasing panels; the provider installs, maintains, and operates the system while charging a fee based on energy consumption or performance. Similarly, microgrid-as-a-service models supply localized renewable power to communities or industrial parks, ensuring reliability and resilience while avoiding upfront infrastructure costs.

Digital technologies underpin the success of service-based models by enabling precision monitoring and performance optimization. Smart meters, Internet of Things (IoT) devices, and data analytics track system performance in real time, allowing providers to identify inefficiencies, predict maintenance needs, and optimize energy delivery. Artificial intelligence supports predictive modeling and demand forecasting, ensuring that systems operate efficiently while maintaining service reliability. Blockchain technology can facilitate transparent contracts and transactions, enabling automated billing and verification of renewable energy generation. These tools make service-based systems more transparent, accountable, and responsive.

Circularity is embedded in service-based models through lifecycle thinking and asset management. Because providers retain ownership of equipment, they have a vested interest in extending its lifespan, designing for easy maintenance, and recovering materials at end of life. Components such as batteries, turbines, or solar panels can be refurbished, repurposed, or recycled for future use, minimizing material waste. This contrasts with linear ownership models, where equipment is often discarded once it becomes obsolete or fails. By maintaining control over assets, service providers create closed material loops that reinforce resource efficiency and sustainability.

Policy and financial mechanisms are evolving to support the growth of service-based business models. Governments can encourage adoption through supportive regulations, tax incentives, and public procurement policies that favor performance-based contracts. Energy regulators can update market structures to accommodate service-oriented transactions, ensuring fair pricing and competition. Financial institutions are increasingly recognizing the stability of long-term service contracts and developing tailored financing instruments for EaaS projects. These policy and financial innovations create enabling environments for scaling circular service models across sectors.

Shifting from ownership to service-based systems redefines the relationship between energy providers and consumers, creating partnerships grounded in performance and sustainability. This model not only supports the integration of renewable energy and digital innovation but also embeds circular principles into business operations. By prioritizing outcomes over assets, service-based models help build an energy system that is efficient, adaptable, and regenerative—one where value is measured not by consumption, but by the lasting benefits delivered to people and the planet.

Financing Circular Energy Transitions

Financing circular energy transitions requires innovative financial mechanisms that align capital flows with sustainability, resilience, and long-term value creation. Traditional financing models often favor linear systems that prioritize short-term returns and capital-intensive infrastructure without accounting for lifecycle impacts. In contrast, circular energy transitions demand investment structures that support regeneration, efficiency, and reuse across the energy system. Financial instruments such as green bonds, blended finance, and impact investment play a central role in mobilizing resources for projects that close loops, reduce waste, and accelerate the adoption of renewable and circular technologies.

Green bonds have emerged as a leading tool for financing circular energy initiatives. These debt instruments are issued to fund projects with measurable environmental benefits, such as renewable energy, energy efficiency, and sustainable infrastructure. By linking capital directly to environmentally responsible activities, green bonds create transparency and accountability for both investors and issuers. Investors gain confidence through clear reporting on environmental outcomes, while issuers benefit from access to lower-cost financing and an expanded investor base. In the context of circular energy systems, green bonds can fund activities like renewable generation upgrades, battery recycling facilities, waste-to-energy plants, or the retrofitting of existing infrastructure for energy efficiency. As green bond markets mature, standardized frameworks and certification schemes—such as those under the Green Bond Principles—help ensure credibility and consistency across projects.

Blended finance complements green bonds by leveraging public and philanthropic capital to mobilize private investment in circular energy transitions. Circular energy projects often face higher upfront costs, longer payback periods, or perceived risks due to emerging technologies and uncertain policy environments. Blended finance mechanisms reduce these barriers by using concessional capital to de-risk investments, making them more attractive to private investors. Public funds may provide guarantees, first-loss tranches, or co-investment structures to absorb potential risks. For example, a government-backed facility might fund the initial development phase of a circular energy project—such as a district heating network or industrial symbiosis hub—while private investors finance the expansion phase. This shared-risk approach enables large-scale implementation of projects that would otherwise remain underfunded.

Impact investment adds another dimension to financing circular energy systems by explicitly linking financial returns to measurable social and environmental outcomes. Impact investors seek to generate positive, quantifiable change while achieving financial sustainability. In the energy sector, this can involve investing in renewable microgrids, circular battery supply chains, or energy-as-a-service models that improve access and efficiency. Measurement frameworks such as the Global Impact Investing Network's (GIIN) IRIS+ system provide standardized metrics for assessing outcomes related to carbon reduction, resource efficiency, and community benefits. As transparency improves, impact investment increasingly channels private capital toward initiatives that advance circularity and support equitable energy transitions.

Financial innovation is also extending to hybrid instruments that combine features of traditional debt and equity with sustainability-linked performance criteria. Sustainability-linked loans and bonds, for instance, tie interest rates or repayment terms to environmental performance indicators, such as energy efficiency improvements or emissions reductions. This alignment of financial incentives with sustainability outcomes encourages companies to continuously improve their circular practices. Similarly, revenue-sharing models and pay-for-performance contracts in energy service systems reward efficiency and resource conservation, reinforcing the economic logic of circularity.

Institutional investors and development banks play a critical role in scaling finance for circular energy systems. Multilateral development banks (MDBs) and national development finance institutions (DFIs) can use their capital and expertise to catalyze private investment through co-financing, technical assistance, and project preparation support. Institutional investors—such as pension funds and insurance companies—are increasingly integrating environmental, social, and governance (ESG) criteria into their portfolios, driving demand for circular and renewable energy assets that offer long-term stability. Platforms for green finance, including climate investment funds and carbon markets, further expand the pool of available capital.

Policy and regulatory frameworks are essential to enable effective financing of circular energy transitions. Governments can introduce tax incentives, credit guarantees, and public procurement programs that prioritize circular solutions. Clear definitions of eligible circular activities and robust monitoring systems increase investor confidence. Collaboration between financial institutions, industry, and policymakers can help align risk assessment methodologies and develop standardized tools for evaluating circular investments.

Financing the circular energy transition requires a shift from short-term profit orientation to long-term value creation. Green bonds, blended finance, and impact investment collectively provide the means to mobilize capital at scale while embedding environmental and social accountability into financial systems. By aligning financial innovation with circular principles, these instruments transform investment from a driver of resource depletion into a catalyst for regeneration—supporting the development of energy systems that are efficient, inclusive, and resilient.

Valuing Externalities and Resource Efficiency

Internalizing environmental externalities is essential to creating sustainable and circular market systems. Externalities—costs or benefits of economic activity that are not reflected in market prices—are a major cause of resource inefficiency and environmental degradation. When the true environmental costs of production, consumption, and disposal are excluded from economic decisions, markets misallocate resources, encouraging waste and overuse. By integrating these costs into pricing mechanisms and investment decisions, societies can promote behaviors that align economic activity with ecological boundaries and long-term sustainability.

Environmental externalities are most evident in the energy sector, where pollution, greenhouse gas emissions, and ecosystem damage often go unpriced. Fossil fuel-based energy systems, for example, impose costs on society through air pollution, climate change, and health impacts that are not borne by producers or consumers. This price distortion favors resource-intensive and polluting activities over cleaner alternatives. Valuing externalities corrects this imbalance by assigning a monetary value to environmental impacts, ensuring that market prices reflect true costs and benefits. Such valuation encourages efficiency, innovation, and the adoption of renewable and circular solutions.

Carbon pricing is one of the most effective tools for internalizing environmental externalities. Through mechanisms such as carbon taxes or emissions trading systems, governments assign a cost to emitting carbon dioxide and other greenhouse gases. This economic signal incentivizes companies to reduce emissions, invest in cleaner technologies, and adopt energy-efficient practices. Carbon pricing also generates revenue that can be reinvested in renewable energy, infrastructure retrofits, and social programs to support equitable transitions. By embedding the environmental cost of carbon into the market, this policy aligns financial and environmental performance, making sustainable energy solutions more competitive.

Beyond carbon, internalizing externalities requires valuing a broader set of environmental impacts, including water use, air pollution, biodiversity loss, and waste generation. Lifecycle-based pricing frameworks can incorporate these externalities by evaluating the full resource and emissions footprint of products and services. For example, differential tariffs on electricity can reflect the environmental intensity of generation sources, encouraging consumers to favor renewable options. Similarly, pollution charges on industrial waste and effluent discharge motivate industries to invest in cleaner production processes. By linking environmental performance to financial outcomes, these approaches reinforce circular behaviors across supply chains.

Resource efficiency is closely tied to the valuation of externalities. When resources are underpriced due to unaccounted environmental costs, wasteful consumption becomes economically rational. Correcting these distortions through pricing and regulation promotes efficiency in production and use. Companies are encouraged to design products with longer lifespans, optimize processes to reduce waste, and adopt closed-loop material systems. Consumers, facing more accurate price signals, are more likely to choose efficient, low-impact goods and services. Over time, this systemic shift reduces demand for virgin materials, lowers emissions, and strengthens economic resilience.

Economic instruments such as taxes, subsidies, and tradable permits are key tools for valuing externalities and promoting resource efficiency. Environmental taxes and levies impose costs on activities that generate pollution or waste, while removing subsidies that encourage resource-intensive behavior ensures fair competition for sustainable alternatives. Tradable permit systems, such as water rights or emissions allowances, create markets for scarce resources, promoting efficiency through price-based allocation. Conversely, subsidies and tax credits for circular technologies—such as energy-efficient equipment, recycling facilities, and renewable generation—reward innovation and accelerate adoption. These financial mechanisms collectively drive a transition toward markets that value sustainability as a core principle.

Corporate accounting and reporting frameworks are evolving to capture the value of externalities and resource efficiency. Environmental, social, and governance (ESG) standards encourage businesses to disclose their environmental impacts and resource use, while emerging methodologies such as natural capital accounting quantify ecosystem services and environmental liabilities. Integrating these measures into financial statements allows investors and regulators to assess corporate performance beyond traditional profit metrics. Over time, this transparency fosters accountability and shifts capital toward organizations that prioritize efficiency and environmental responsibility.

Policy frameworks and international cooperation strengthen the valuation of externalities across markets. Governments can implement comprehensive environmental pricing systems, establish standards for ecological valuation, and harmonize methodologies across borders. Coordination between countries reduces the risk of competitive disadvantages for early adopters and supports global progress toward sustainability goals. International institutions and development banks can assist by funding capacity-building programs, developing valuation tools, and supporting implementation in emerging economies.

Valuing externalities and promoting resource efficiency transform the economic foundation of energy and production systems. By integrating environmental costs into market structures, pricing signals reflect true scarcity and ecological value. This approach not only encourages innovation and sustainable investment but also ensures that economic growth aligns with planetary limits. When markets internalize the cost of environmental degradation, they become instruments of regeneration—rewarding efficiency, circularity, and responsible stewardship of resources.

Incentives, Regulations, and Carbon Pricing

Public policy plays a pivotal role in steering private investment toward sustainable and circular energy systems. Market forces alone often fail to account for environmental externalities or provide sufficient incentives for long-term, low-carbon investments. To address these gaps, governments employ a combination of incentives, regulations, and carbon pricing mechanisms that align private sector behavior with public sustainability objectives. These policy tools encourage innovation, de-risk investments, and create stable conditions for the development of renewable energy and circular economy practices.

Incentives are among the most direct methods for accelerating private investment in sustainable energy. They reduce financial barriers, encourage technology adoption, and make early-stage circular initiatives more competitive. Fiscal incentives such as tax credits, accelerated depreciation, and investment allowances help lower the capital costs of renewable energy projects, energy efficiency upgrades, and recycling infrastructure. For instance, feed-in tariffs guarantee fixed payments for renewable electricity generation, providing long-term revenue certainty. Similarly, production tax credits and grants for clean technologies encourage companies to invest in research, development, and deployment of innovative solutions. On the consumer side, rebates and low-interest financing for energy-efficient appliances, electric vehicles, and rooftop solar systems expand market participation and stimulate demand for sustainable products.

Public procurement also functions as an incentive by creating stable markets for sustainable solutions. Governments can set circular procurement policies that prioritize products with low embodied carbon, high recyclability, or certified environmental performance. By leveraging their purchasing power, public institutions signal demand for circular goods and services, encouraging industries to align their production and design practices with sustainability standards. This approach not only reduces the environmental footprint of public spending but also supports the scaling of emerging circular business models.

Regulations complement incentives by setting mandatory standards that ensure compliance and consistency across sectors. Environmental regulations establish performance benchmarks for emissions, energy efficiency, and waste management, creating a level playing field for responsible companies. Building codes requiring energy-efficient construction, vehicle emission standards, and renewable portfolio standards for utilities are examples of regulatory measures that drive systemic change. In the context of the circular energy economy, regulations can also mandate extended producer responsibility, requiring manufacturers to manage the end-of-life recovery of their products. Such frameworks encourage design for durability, reuse, and recyclability, embedding circularity directly into production systems.

Well-designed regulations promote innovation rather than stifling it. By providing clear, predictable, and progressively tightening standards, policymakers enable businesses to plan long-term investments with confidence. Regulatory flexibility—through mechanisms such as tradable permits or performance-based standards—allows companies to achieve compliance in the most cost-effective ways. For example, cap-and-trade systems for pollutants enable firms to buy and sell emission allowances, rewarding those that exceed efficiency targets while maintaining overall environmental integrity.

Carbon pricing serves as one of the most powerful tools for aligning private investment with public climate goals. By assigning an economic cost to greenhouse gas emissions, carbon pricing internalizes environmental externalities, ensuring that market prices reflect true social and environmental costs. There are two primary approaches: carbon taxes and emissions trading systems (ETS). Carbon taxes set a fixed price per ton of emissions, providing price certainty for businesses and encouraging gradual decarbonization. ETS, by contrast, cap total emissions and allow the market to determine the price of carbon through trading. Both mechanisms incentivize low-carbon innovation, improve resource efficiency, and make cleaner technologies more competitive relative to fossil-based alternatives.

Revenues from carbon pricing can further accelerate circular energy transitions when reinvested strategically. Funds can support renewable energy deployment, energy efficiency retrofits, low-income household transitions, and research into carbon capture and circular technologies. Revenue recycling also mitigates potential social impacts by offsetting energy cost increases for vulnerable populations. When integrated with complementary policies, carbon pricing creates a coherent policy environment where financial, social, and environmental objectives reinforce one another.

Policy coherence is critical to maximizing the effectiveness of incentives, regulations, and pricing mechanisms. Fragmented or inconsistent policy frameworks can create uncertainty and deter investment. Aligning fiscal policy, environmental regulation, and industrial strategy ensures that incentives reward genuine sustainability outcomes rather than short-term compliance. Coordination across ministries and between national and local governments supports the scaling of circular energy systems through aligned objectives and shared data frameworks.

International cooperation strengthens the impact of domestic policy tools. Harmonizing carbon pricing systems, establishing shared environmental standards, and coordinating green finance initiatives prevent competitive imbalances and promote global investment flows. Development banks and multilateral funds can provide technical and financial support to help emerging economies adopt and implement effective incentive and regulatory frameworks.

Incentives, regulations, and carbon pricing together form a balanced policy mix that integrates economic and environmental objectives. Incentives stimulate innovation and investment, regulations ensure accountability and consistency, and carbon pricing embeds environmental costs into market structures. When designed cohesively, these instruments not only guide private capital toward sustainability but also foster a resilient, efficient, and equitable energy system that reflects the true value of environmental stewardship.

Chapter 7: Policy, Governance, and Institutional Frameworks

Policy, governance, and institutional frameworks provide the structural foundation for advancing circular energy systems. Effective governance ensures coherence among economic, environmental, and social objectives while enabling innovation and accountability. This chapter explores how national strategies, regulatory systems, and institutional coordination support the circular energy transition. It examines the role of policies in fostering investment, aligning incentives, and integrating lifecycle accountability. By highlighting multi-level governance, public-private collaboration, and international cooperation, the chapter demonstrates how institutional design translates circular principles into practical, enforceable mechanisms for achieving sustainable and resilient energy systems.

National and Regional Circular Energy Policies

National and regional circular energy policies are reshaping how governments plan and manage their energy transitions. As countries seek to achieve decarbonization, resource efficiency, and energy security simultaneously, embedding circularity into policy frameworks has become a strategic imperative. Circular energy policies move beyond simply promoting renewable energy; they aim to redesign the entire energy system to minimize waste, optimize resource use, and maximize value retention across lifecycles. These frameworks integrate environmental, industrial, and social objectives, ensuring that the transition to sustainable energy systems contributes to long-term economic resilience.

At the national level, circular energy policies often emerge as part of broader climate or green growth strategies. Governments recognize that achieving carbon neutrality requires more than switching to renewables—it also demands transforming how energy infrastructure, industries, and consumption patterns interact. National energy plans increasingly include circular objectives such as promoting energy efficiency, supporting material recovery from renewable technologies, and incentivizing industrial symbiosis. Countries with advanced climate legislation often incorporate circular principles through measures like extended producer responsibility for renewable energy components, mandatory lifecycle assessments, and funding programs for waste-to-energy innovation. These initiatives ensure that new energy technologies do not create future waste or resource challenges.

Circular energy policies also focus on integrating sectors that traditionally operated in isolation. Energy, transport, agriculture, and waste management are being linked through resource loops that enhance overall efficiency. For example, national policies promoting bioenergy production often couple agricultural waste utilization with renewable heat generation and nutrient recovery. Similarly, integrating waste-to-energy systems into municipal waste frameworks reduces landfill volumes while generating renewable power. This systemic approach allows national governments to address multiple sustainability challenges—emissions, waste, and resource depletion—through unified policy action.

Regional policies play a critical role in implementing and adapting circular energy principles to local contexts. Regions often have distinct resource bases, industrial structures, and energy needs, requiring tailored approaches to circularity. Regional authorities can promote industrial symbiosis, where energy, materials, and by-products are exchanged between facilities within an industrial cluster. For instance, waste heat from one plant may be used to supply district heating to nearby communities, while recovered materials from one industry feed into another's production process. These localized networks strengthen regional economies, reduce emissions, and enhance resilience by optimizing resource use within geographic proximity.

The European Union has been a global leader in embedding circularity into energy and climate policy. Its Circular Economy Action Plan and Green Deal integrate circular principles into renewable energy, mobility, and industrial strategy. The EU's focus on resource efficiency, eco-design, and energy system integration sets a benchmark for policy coherence. Instruments such as the Renewable Energy Directive, the Energy Efficiency Directive, and the Industrial Emissions Directive collectively ensure that circularity is not an isolated goal but a cross-cutting element of the energy transition. Similar regional frameworks are emerging elsewhere, such as the African Union's Agenda 2063, which highlights circular resource management, and ASEAN's regional strategies promoting clean energy and sustainable industrial development.

Policy coherence across national and regional levels is essential for effective circular energy governance. National frameworks provide strategic direction and long-term targets, while regional and local authorities translate these into context-specific implementation. Coordination mechanisms—such as shared data systems, harmonized standards, and multi-level governance platforms—ensure alignment and avoid duplication of efforts. Regional innovation clusters and pilot projects serve as testbeds for new circular energy technologies and business models, generating knowledge that can inform national strategies.

Financing and capacity-building are integral to successful implementation of circular energy policies. National governments can establish dedicated funds for circular energy innovation and provide fiscal incentives for companies investing in circular practices. Regional authorities can facilitate partnerships between academia, industry, and local governments to foster skills development and technology transfer. Integrating circularity into public procurement and infrastructure investment also ensures that government spending supports sustainable outcomes.

As nations and regions continue to revise their energy strategies, circularity provides a unifying framework for balancing economic development with environmental stewardship. By embedding circular principles into policy design, governments create systems that conserve resources, foster innovation, and maintain long-term energy resilience. National and regional circular energy policies thus represent a structural shift toward sustainability—transforming the way societies produce, distribute, and consume energy in harmony with ecological and economic limits.

Regulatory Innovation and Standards

Regulatory innovation and standards are vital for embedding circularity into the energy sector, ensuring that products, infrastructure, and processes align with principles of resource recovery, efficiency, and lifecycle accountability. Traditional regulatory systems were designed for linear models of production and consumption, focusing primarily on environmental compliance and pollution control. As economies transition toward circular energy systems, regulations are evolving to encourage innovation, guide product design, and mandate responsibility throughout the entire lifecycle of energy technologies. These frameworks create the conditions necessary for sustainable markets, fostering long-term investment in regenerative and resource-efficient solutions.

Modern regulatory systems promote circularity by shifting from end-of-pipe environmental management to lifecycle-based governance. Instead of regulating only emissions or waste disposal, policymakers now address upstream design, material selection, and system integration. Regulations that mandate eco-design and lifecycle assessment ensure that products and technologies minimize environmental impact from the earliest stages of development. For example, energy equipment such as batteries, solar panels, and wind turbines must increasingly comply with design requirements that enable reuse, repair, and recycling. These design-oriented regulations help prevent waste generation and reduce dependence on virgin materials by keeping components and resources circulating within the economy.

Extended Producer Responsibility (EPR) schemes are one of the most effective regulatory innovations for achieving lifecycle accountability. Under EPR, manufacturers retain responsibility for their products even after sale, including end-of-life collection, treatment, and recycling. This approach shifts the financial and

78

logistical burden of waste management away from governments and toward producers, incentivizing them to design products that are easier to disassemble and recycle. In the energy sector, EPR is being applied to photovoltaic panels, energy storage systems, and electronic components, ensuring that valuable materials such as lithium, rare earth elements, and aluminum are recovered and reused. By linking accountability with design, EPR fosters circular innovation across entire supply chains.

Standards play a critical role in operationalizing regulatory goals and ensuring consistency across industries and markets. Technical standards establish benchmarks for resource efficiency, recyclability, and product durability, helping manufacturers and investors align with circular principles. Lifecycle standards, such as ISO 14040 and ISO 14044 for Life Cycle Assessment, provide methodologies for evaluating environmental impacts across product lifecycles. Standards for material recovery and recycling efficiency ensure that recovered resources meet quality requirements for reuse, supporting secondary material markets. Consistent, science-based standards reduce uncertainty, promote transparency, and create a level playing field for companies adopting circular practices.

Regulatory innovation also encourages collaboration between public authorities, industry, and research institutions to develop and test new circular solutions. Pilot regulatory frameworks, sometimes known as "regulatory sandboxes," allow experimentation with emerging technologies and business models in controlled environments. These initiatives help policymakers understand potential barriers and refine regulations to better support innovation. For instance, sandboxes for renewable hydrogen production, smart grid management, or waste-to-energy systems enable developers to test circular models before broad implementation. Such adaptive regulation accelerates technological development while maintaining environmental integrity.

Digital technologies are increasingly integrated into regulatory systems to enhance lifecycle accountability and traceability. Blockchain and digital product passports enable tracking of materials and components throughout production, use, and end-of-life phases. Regulators can use these tools to verify compliance, monitor recycling performance, and ensure that recovered materials meet quality standards. Digital traceability also supports transparent reporting, enabling consumers and investors to make informed decisions based on verified sustainability data.

International cooperation is essential for harmonizing regulatory innovation and standards across borders. Energy supply chains are global, and inconsistent regulations can create market distortions or hinder the flow of circular materials. Collaborative initiatives, such as the European Union's Circular Economy Action Plan and the United Nations' Sustainable Development Goals, promote shared frameworks for circular product design, recycling standards, and resource recovery. Harmonized certification systems and mutual recognition of standards reduce transaction costs and enable the global scaling of circular energy solutions.

The evolution of regulatory systems toward innovation and lifecycle accountability represents a fundamental shift in governance philosophy. Rather than simply limiting environmental harm, modern regulations actively promote circular design, resource recovery, and technological advancement. Through extended producer responsibility, adaptive regulation, and harmonized standards, governments can create an enabling environment where circularity becomes the norm. These measures ensure that the energy transition not only reduces emissions but also conserves resources, fosters innovation, and builds resilience within a sustainable global economy.

Institutional Coordination and Multi-Level Governance

Institutional coordination and multi-level governance are essential components of effective circular energy transitions. The shift toward a circular energy economy involves complex interactions across different sectors, jurisdictions, and scales of governance. Local, regional, and national authorities each hold distinct responsibilities for planning, implementation, and regulation. Without clear coordination, fragmented decision-making can lead to inefficiencies, policy overlaps, and missed opportunities for systemic integration. Multi-level governance frameworks create the mechanisms necessary to align objectives, streamline implementation, and ensure that circular energy initiatives function cohesively across all levels of administration.

At the national level, governments set the overarching strategic direction for circular energy transitions through legislation, targets, and funding mechanisms. National energy and climate strategies define long-term goals, such as net-zero emissions or renewable energy capacity expansion, while integrating circular economy principles related to resource efficiency, waste minimization, and material recovery. Ministries of energy, environment, industry, and finance often share responsibility for implementing these goals. Effective coordination among these institutions prevents policy conflicts and fosters integrated planning. Inter-ministerial committees or national councils for sustainable development provide platforms for collaboration, ensuring that circular objectives are embedded across all relevant policy domains.

Regional authorities act as intermediaries between national frameworks and local implementation. Their role includes adapting national policies to regional contexts, managing energy infrastructure, and promoting industrial symbiosis. Regions often possess the regulatory authority to oversee energy distribution networks, renewable project permitting, and waste-to-energy systems. Regional energy agencies and development boards serve as coordination hubs, connecting municipalities, industries, and community organizations. These entities facilitate resource sharing, data exchange, and technical assistance, ensuring that circular energy policies align with regional economic and environmental priorities. By managing the spatial dimension of energy systems, regional governance helps balance local needs with national objectives.

Local governments play a crucial role as implementers and innovators in circular energy governance. Cities and municipalities are responsible for managing waste, water, and local energy systems—sectors central to circularity. They are also the primary interface with citizens, enabling behavioral change and community participation in energy efficiency programs, recycling schemes, and renewable deployment. Local authorities can drive innovation through urban planning policies that promote energy-efficient buildings, district heating systems, and renewable microgrids. Local pilot projects often serve as testing grounds for national strategies, demonstrating scalable models for resource recovery and circular infrastructure. However, the success of these initiatives depends on strong coordination mechanisms that connect local actions to broader policy frameworks.

Effective multi-level governance requires clear communication channels and collaborative structures that align decision-making across administrative levels. Vertical coordination ensures that local and regional efforts reinforce national objectives, while horizontal coordination promotes collaboration among institutions operating at the same level. National governments can facilitate this process by establishing shared data platforms, standardized reporting systems, and joint planning mechanisms. For example, integrated resource management plans developed collaboratively by local and regional authorities ensure coherence in land use, water management, and energy infrastructure. Regular policy dialogues and intergovernmental working groups further strengthen coordination and build institutional capacity for circular energy governance.

Institutional coordination also depends on financial and technical alignment. National governments provide funding and policy incentives, while regional and local entities implement projects and manage operations. Multi-level financing arrangements—such as co-funding schemes, green investment platforms, and regional development funds—help bridge resource gaps between jurisdictions. Technical assistance programs and knowledge-sharing networks enable subnational authorities to access expertise, best practices, and technologies needed to implement circular energy initiatives. These collaborative frameworks enhance policy coherence and promote equitable access to resources across different regions and municipalities.

Governance innovation is increasingly supported by digitalization and data integration. Smart governance platforms enable real-time monitoring of energy and resource flows, facilitating coordination across levels of government. Geographic information systems (GIS) and digital twins allow decision-makers to visualize infrastructure, resource networks, and emissions data in integrated ways. Data-driven governance improves transparency, accountability, and responsiveness, ensuring that circular energy policies are informed by accurate and timely information. Digital platforms also support public engagement, allowing citizens and businesses to contribute to monitoring progress and shaping local initiatives.

International experience highlights the value of institutionalized coordination mechanisms. The European Union's multi-level governance model, for example, integrates national energy and climate plans with regional and local implementation through structured reporting and funding frameworks. Similar models are being developed in federal systems such as Canada and Germany, where provinces and states play central roles in managing energy transitions while adhering to national climate goals. These systems demonstrate how governance alignment fosters innovation, efficiency, and long-term policy stability.

Multi-level governance also enhances inclusivity and legitimacy in decision-making. Engaging diverse stakeholders—from industry and academia to civil society and local communities—ensures that circular energy transitions reflect shared priorities and social realities. Collaborative governance models based on partnerships and co-creation build public trust and strengthen accountability. This participatory approach not only improves policy effectiveness but also reinforces social cohesion by making the energy transition a collective endeavor.

Institutional coordination and multi-level governance transform fragmented energy policy landscapes into cohesive systems capable of delivering circular outcomes. By aligning strategies, resources, and responsibilities across jurisdictions, these governance structures enable the efficient and equitable implementation of circular energy principles. The result is a more adaptive, integrated, and resilient governance framework that supports sustainable energy transitions at every scale—from local innovation to national leadership.

Public-Private Partnerships and Stakeholder Collaboration

Public-private partnerships (PPPs) and stakeholder collaboration are essential mechanisms for financing, developing, and scaling circular energy systems. The complexity of transitioning to a circular energy economy—characterized by renewable integration, resource recovery, and lifecycle management—requires coordinated action across governments, businesses, investors, and civil society. No single actor possesses the resources or expertise to achieve this transformation alone. Collaborative frameworks such as PPPs enable the pooling of financial, technical, and institutional capacities, while multi-stakeholder engagement ensures that circular initiatives are socially inclusive, economically viable, and environmentally sustainable.

PPPs are formalized cooperative arrangements between public authorities and private entities designed to deliver infrastructure and services traditionally provided by the public sector. In the context of circular energy systems, these partnerships finance, construct, and manage projects such as renewable power plants, waste-to-energy facilities, district heating networks, and smart grids. Governments typically provide regulatory support, access to land, and risk mitigation instruments, while private partners contribute investment capital, innovation, and operational expertise. This shared-risk, shared-benefit model allows governments to leverage private sector efficiency and innovation while maintaining public oversight of strategic assets.

Financing circular energy projects often involves high upfront costs and long payback periods, making PPPs particularly valuable for attracting investment. Through mechanisms such as long-term concession agreements, performance-based contracts, and revenue-sharing models, PPPs provide investors with predictable returns while ensuring that projects align with public sustainability objectives. For example, energy performance contracting allows private firms to finance and manage energy efficiency upgrades in public buildings, with repayment linked to verified energy savings. Similarly, waste-to-energy PPPs can operate under build-own-operate-transfer (BOOT) models, where the private partner develops and manages facilities for a defined period before transferring ownership to the public sector. These structures promote accountability, transparency, and long-term resource efficiency.

Policy frameworks play a critical role in creating an enabling environment for PPPs. Governments can establish clear guidelines, standardized contract templates, and regulatory stability to reduce transaction risks and attract private investment. Green procurement policies that prioritize circular criteria—such as lifecycle performance, resource recovery, and low-carbon materials—further stimulate demand for circular solutions. Additionally, public guarantees, credit enhancements, and blended finance instruments can lower financial risks for investors entering emerging circular markets. By combining public support with private innovation, PPPs can unlock large-scale funding for energy systems that are both resilient and regenerative.

Stakeholder collaboration extends beyond formal PPPs to include diverse actors involved in the circular energy transition. Utilities, technology providers, financial institutions, academia, and civil society each contribute unique perspectives and resources. Multi-stakeholder platforms facilitate dialogue, coordination, and knowledge exchange, ensuring that policies and projects reflect shared priorities. These platforms often operate at national and regional levels, bringing together policymakers, businesses, and community representatives to align goals and overcome implementation challenges. Such collaboration is crucial for integrating circular principles across sectors and for ensuring that innovation translates into practical, scalable solutions.

Local governments and communities play a vital role in stakeholder collaboration by ensuring that circular energy projects meet social and environmental needs. Community energy initiatives, for example, demonstrate how collective ownership models can complement PPP structures. In these models, local residents invest in and co-manage renewable or efficiency projects, keeping economic benefits within the community. This participatory approach strengthens public trust, encourages behavioral change, and enhances project acceptance. Similarly, partnerships between municipalities and local businesses can promote industrial symbiosis, where energy and material by-products are exchanged to improve efficiency and reduce waste.

Research institutions and universities contribute to collaborative frameworks by providing data, analysis, and technological innovation. Through public-private research partnerships, new materials, storage systems, and circular technologies are developed and tested. These collaborations bridge the gap between policy and practice, enabling the continuous refinement of strategies and solutions. Knowledge transfer from academia to industry accelerates innovation and supports evidence-based policymaking.

Transparent communication and stakeholder engagement are also fundamental to successful collaboration. Open data platforms and consultation processes ensure that project impacts and benefits are clearly understood. Early and continuous stakeholder involvement minimizes conflict, enhances accountability, and allows adaptive management based on feedback. Digital collaboration tools further strengthen coordination, enabling real-time information sharing among partners involved in planning, financing, and implementation.

International collaboration adds another layer to PPP and stakeholder networks, allowing countries to share best practices, harmonize standards, and mobilize transnational financing. Global initiatives—

such as those led by development banks, international agencies, and climate funds—provide technical assistance and funding support for circular energy PPPs in developing regions. Cross-border partnerships facilitate technology transfer and knowledge exchange, helping to replicate successful models across diverse contexts.

Public-private partnerships and stakeholder collaboration create the institutional foundation for advancing circular energy systems. By combining the innovation and efficiency of the private sector with the strategic vision and accountability of the public sector, these mechanisms mobilize resources and expertise at scale. When complemented by inclusive, transparent stakeholder engagement, PPPs ensure that circular energy transitions deliver economic, social, and environmental value. Through shared governance and mutual commitment, collaboration transforms circular energy from an abstract policy goal into an achievable, system-wide reality.

Chapter 8: Digitalization, Data, and Innovation

Digitalization, data, and innovation underpin the transformation toward circular energy systems. By integrating advanced technologies such as artificial intelligence, the Internet of Things, and blockchain, energy systems become more transparent, efficient, and adaptive. This chapter explores how digital tools enable real-time optimization, traceability, and predictive management across the energy value chain. It also examines the importance of data governance, interoperability, and innovation ecosystems in fostering collaboration and scalability. Through digital integration and continuous innovation, circular energy systems evolve into intelligent networks capable of maximizing efficiency, minimizing waste, and supporting long-term sustainability.

Digital Technologies in Circular Energy Systems

Digital technologies are transforming the structure and performance of circular energy systems by enabling transparency, efficiency, and real-time optimization across energy value chains. Artificial intelligence (AI), the Internet of Things (IoT), and blockchain technologies serve as the backbone of this transformation, integrating data, devices, and decision-making into a cohesive, adaptive network. These technologies not only enhance system performance but also ensure that circular principles—resource recovery, efficiency, and lifecycle accountability—are embedded throughout the energy system.

AI enables intelligent management of complex energy networks by analyzing vast datasets to identify patterns, predict trends, and optimize operations. In renewable energy generation, AI algorithms forecast solar and wind output by processing meteorological and sensor data, improving accuracy in supply predictions and reducing curtailment. Predictive analytics also enhance grid stability by anticipating fluctuations in demand and optimizing power distribution. For circular energy systems, AI supports resource efficiency through dynamic energy management, optimizing when and how resources are used. It facilitates lifecycle planning by analyzing maintenance data to extend asset life and by improving recycling processes through material sorting and predictive quality assessment.

The IoT underpins digitalization by connecting physical infrastructure—such as power plants, storage systems, and consumption devices—into intelligent networks. Smart sensors embedded throughout the energy value chain collect real-time data on performance, temperature, energy flows, and resource usage. This connectivity enables continuous monitoring and control of distributed systems, from individual household appliances to industrial facilities. For example, IoT-enabled smart grids can automatically adjust electricity flows based on renewable generation availability, while IoT-equipped buildings optimize heating, cooling, and lighting to minimize waste. These technologies make circular energy systems adaptive, self-regulating, and responsive to both user behavior and environmental conditions.

AI and IoT work in synergy to improve predictive maintenance and resource utilization. By continuously analyzing sensor data, AI can detect early signs of equipment degradation or inefficiency, prompting timely maintenance that prevents costly failures and extends the lifespan of infrastructure. This predictive approach aligns with circular principles by maximizing asset performance and reducing the need for premature replacement. In industrial systems, IoT data enables the recovery and reuse of waste heat, water, and materials, while AI optimizes their redistribution within industrial symbiosis networks. Together, these technologies transform energy systems from reactive operations into proactive, self-learning ecosystems.

Blockchain technology adds an essential layer of transparency, traceability, and trust to digitalized circular energy systems. It functions as a decentralized ledger that securely records transactions and data exchanges across participants without the need for intermediaries. In energy markets, blockchain enables peer-to-peer trading, where households and businesses can directly buy and sell excess renewable energy. This decentralization democratizes energy systems, reducing inefficiencies and administrative costs. For circular supply chains, blockchain ensures transparency by tracing materials and components throughout their lifecycle—from extraction and manufacturing to use, recycling, and reuse. This traceability supports responsible sourcing and verifies compliance with environmental and social standards.

Blockchain also enhances accountability in carbon management and renewable energy certification. Smart contracts—self-executing digital agreements embedded in blockchain—automate transactions based on predefined sustainability criteria. For instance, energy credits can be automatically issued when renewable generation thresholds are met, ensuring accurate and verifiable reporting. Similarly, carbon offsets or recycling credits can be recorded and traded transparently, fostering trust in environmental markets. By integrating blockchain into energy systems, stakeholders can verify that circular objectives—such as emissions reduction, recycling efficiency, or energy savings—are achieved and documented in real time.

Digital platforms that integrate AI, IoT, and blockchain enable systemic optimization across entire energy ecosystems. These platforms connect generation, distribution, storage, and consumption through unified data architectures, allowing seamless coordination between stakeholders. For instance, AI-driven energy management systems can use blockchain-based smart contracts to execute real-time energy trades between producers and consumers, while IoT sensors ensure accurate measurement and reporting. This interoperability creates efficient, transparent, and adaptive circular systems that minimize losses and maximize renewable use.

Despite their transformative potential, the adoption of digital technologies in circular energy systems requires enabling policies and secure data governance. Governments and regulators can promote digital integration by establishing standards for data sharing, cybersecurity, and interoperability. Investment in digital infrastructure and skills development ensures that both public and private actors can fully leverage emerging technologies. Transparency frameworks and ethical guidelines also ensure that AI and data analytics are used responsibly and inclusively.

Digital technologies create the intelligence layer that allows circular energy systems to function effectively. By combining AI's predictive power, IoT's connectivity, and blockchain's transparency, these tools close information and resource loops across the energy value chain. The result is an energy system that is efficient, resilient, and accountable—capable of adapting dynamically to environmental, technological, and social change while advancing the goals of circularity and sustainability.

Data Governance and Energy Traceability

Data governance and energy traceability are critical foundations of circular energy systems, ensuring that digital transformation supports transparency, accountability, and efficiency across the entire energy value chain. As digital technologies such as artificial intelligence, the Internet of Things, and blockchain increasingly shape how energy is produced, distributed, and consumed, vast quantities of data are generated. Managing this data responsibly and effectively allows stakeholders to make real-time decisions, verify sustainability outcomes, and optimize the use of resources in alignment with circular principles. Robust data governance frameworks establish the rules, standards, and infrastructures that enable trustworthy data exchange while protecting privacy, security, and integrity.

Data governance defines how data is collected, stored, shared, and used within energy systems. It encompasses technical, legal, and institutional dimensions that determine data ownership, access rights, and quality standards. In circular energy systems, data governance ensures that information on resource flows, emissions, and lifecycle performance is accurate and accessible to relevant stakeholders. This transparency allows regulators, investors, and consumers to monitor compliance with sustainability goals and to make evidence-based decisions. For example, tracking energy use and waste recovery across industrial networks enables authorities to assess progress toward circular targets and identify inefficiencies or potential synergies.

High-quality data is central to effective governance. Energy systems increasingly rely on real-time data from sensors, smart meters, and monitoring platforms to manage distributed renewable resources, predict demand, and detect system anomalies. To maintain reliability, governance frameworks must ensure data accuracy, standardization, and interoperability across devices and systems. Common data standards and protocols allow information to flow seamlessly between different technologies and institutions, preventing fragmentation and enabling integration. Without consistent standards, digital innovations such as smart grids, peer-to-peer trading platforms, or lifecycle tracking systems risk operating in isolation, undermining circular efficiency.

Energy traceability builds on strong governance by providing a transparent record of energy and material flows across their entire lifecycle. Traceability systems use digital identifiers, databases, and blockchain ledgers to document the origin, transformation, and destination of energy and associated resources. This capability is particularly important for renewable and circular energy systems, where accountability and trust are essential. For example, traceability ensures that electricity labeled as "green" originates from verifiable renewable sources. It can also document the circular performance of technologies—such as the recovery rate of materials in wind turbines or batteries—enabling companies to demonstrate compliance with environmental and social standards.

Blockchain technology has become a key enabler of traceability by creating tamper-resistant records of energy transactions and material flows. It allows participants in the energy ecosystem to share verified data securely without relying on a central intermediary. Smart contracts embedded within blockchain systems can automate compliance and verification processes—for instance, issuing renewable energy certificates automatically when generation criteria are met. This automation enhances accountability and reduces administrative burdens, making transparency an integral feature of circular energy markets.

Real-time data management enhances decision-making by allowing dynamic responses to changing conditions in the energy system. Predictive analytics powered by AI can interpret incoming data streams from smart grids or distributed energy resources, identifying patterns and recommending actions that optimize efficiency. Operators can balance supply and demand, adjust grid operations, and manage storage systems proactively. At the same time, real-time data enables policymakers and regulators to monitor system performance and adjust policies accordingly, ensuring that regulatory frameworks remain responsive and effective.

Effective data governance frameworks also address privacy, cybersecurity, and ethical concerns. As digital energy systems collect increasingly granular information about consumption patterns, protecting user privacy becomes essential. Governance policies must define who can access data, under what conditions, and for what purposes. Cybersecurity measures safeguard against manipulation or unauthorized access, ensuring that energy traceability data remains reliable. Ethical guidelines further ensure that AI and analytics are applied responsibly, preventing biases or unintended environmental trade-offs.

Collaboration among public institutions, private companies, and technology providers is vital for establishing harmonized governance and traceability systems. Governments can set overarching principles and regulatory requirements for data sharing, while industry consortia and standardization bodies develop technical protocols. International cooperation helps align data frameworks across borders, facilitating cross-border energy trade and global supply chain transparency. Public-private partnerships can also support the creation of digital infrastructure and open data platforms that allow stakeholders to share information efficiently.

Data governance and energy traceability transform information into a strategic asset that supports the functioning of circular energy systems. By ensuring that data is accurate, secure, and accessible, governance frameworks build trust among stakeholders and enable continuous improvement through real-time decision-making. Traceability systems make energy and resource flows visible, verifiable, and accountable, reinforcing the circular principles of transparency and efficiency. Together, they form the informational backbone of sustainable energy transitions—linking digital innovation to environmental integrity and long-term resilience.

Predictive Analytics and Resource Optimization

Predictive analytics and resource optimization form the analytical foundation of circular energy systems. By harnessing large datasets and applying advanced algorithms, these tools enable decision-makers to anticipate trends, identify inefficiencies, and allocate resources more effectively. Predictive models allow energy systems to move from reactive to proactive management—reducing waste, improving reliability, and maximizing the use of renewable resources. In a circular energy economy, data-driven forecasting not only enhances operational efficiency but also supports long-term sustainability by aligning energy production, consumption, and resource flows within environmental limits.

Predictive analytics uses statistical modeling, machine learning, and artificial intelligence (AI) to analyze historical and real-time data, generating insights into future performance. In the energy sector, predictive tools forecast electricity demand, renewable generation, equipment maintenance needs, and market trends. These forecasts allow operators to plan production schedules, balance grids, and optimize storage systems. For example, AI algorithms can predict solar or wind generation based on weather data, enabling utilities to adjust grid operations and minimize curtailment. This foresight ensures that renewable energy is used efficiently and that excess power is stored or redirected when supply exceeds demand.

Resource optimization complements predictive analytics by using the insights generated from data to allocate energy, materials, and assets more effectively. Optimization tools model complex systems—such as interconnected grids, industrial networks, and supply chains—to determine how resources can be used most efficiently under varying conditions. In circular energy systems, optimization focuses not only on cost and performance but also on minimizing environmental impact and maximizing resource recovery. By integrating predictive forecasts with optimization models, operators can coordinate renewable generation, storage, and demand response in real time, achieving a balance between efficiency and sustainability.

One of the most impactful applications of predictive analytics is in energy demand forecasting. Accurate demand prediction enables utilities to match production with consumption, reducing energy waste and avoiding reliance on carbon-intensive backup generation. Advanced models combine historical consumption patterns with contextual data such as temperature, population growth, and economic activity. Machine learning algorithms continuously refine these forecasts by learning from deviations and incorporating new variables. Demand-side management programs use these insights to encourage consumers to shift usage to periods of high renewable availability, improving grid flexibility and stability.

Predictive maintenance represents another key area where analytics enhances circular efficiency. By continuously monitoring equipment through sensors and IoT networks, predictive algorithms identify signs of wear, vibration anomalies, or temperature fluctuations that indicate potential failures. Maintenance can then be scheduled precisely when needed, preventing costly breakdowns and extending the lifespan of assets. This approach aligns with circular principles by reducing material waste, avoiding unplanned downtime, and minimizing energy losses associated with inefficient operation. For example, predictive maintenance in wind farms ensures that turbines operate at peak efficiency, while in industrial plants, it helps recover waste heat and improve overall energy performance.

In industrial and manufacturing contexts, predictive analytics and optimization enable resource loops that enhance circularity. Process optimization models analyze production data to minimize energy use, water consumption, and material waste. By simulating different process configurations, these models identify opportunities for energy recovery, waste heat utilization, or by-product exchange with nearby facilities. When combined with real-time monitoring, predictive tools allow industries to adapt to changing conditions dynamically, maintaining efficiency without compromising productivity. This adaptability supports industrial symbiosis, where multiple facilities collaborate to share energy and material flows, forming closed-loop systems that reduce environmental footprints.

Predictive analytics also strengthens renewable energy integration by addressing intermittency challenges. Hybrid optimization models coordinate multiple storage and generation technologies—such as solar, wind, batteries, and hydrogen—to ensure continuous power supply. Forecasting algorithms predict renewable output and adjust storage and demand accordingly. For example, during periods of high solar generation, predictive tools can trigger battery charging or hydrogen production, storing energy for later use. During low generation periods, these stored resources are dispatched strategically to maintain grid reliability. This integrated, data-driven approach enhances resource efficiency while supporting the decarbonization of energy systems.

At the urban scale, predictive analytics supports smart city energy management. Integrated data platforms analyze information from buildings, transport networks, and public infrastructure to optimize energy flows. Predictive models forecast electricity use across neighborhoods, allowing for better distribution and integration of renewable sources. Optimization algorithms manage public lighting, electric vehicle charging, and heating systems to minimize demand peaks. Cities can use these insights to plan infrastructure investments, reduce emissions, and improve resilience to energy fluctuations.

The effectiveness of predictive analytics and resource optimization depends on robust data governance and interoperability. High-quality, standardized data ensures that models are accurate and comparable across systems. Collaboration between public institutions, private companies, and research organizations enhances model development and validation. Open data initiatives and digital platforms enable wider access to predictive tools, supporting capacity building and innovation. Policymakers can further encourage adoption by funding digital infrastructure, establishing regulatory frameworks for data sharing, and incentivizing the integration of analytics into energy planning.

Predictive analytics and resource optimization represent a convergence of data science and sustainability. By transforming data into actionable intelligence, these tools allow energy systems to anticipate needs, minimize waste, and adapt to variability. They transform static infrastructure into dynamic, learning systems capable of continuous improvement. Within the circular energy economy, predictive intelligence ensures that resources are used not only efficiently but also responsibly—balancing human needs with environmental limits while supporting a resilient, low-carbon future.

Innovation Ecosystems and Technological Diffusion

Innovation ecosystems and technological diffusion are central to advancing circular energy solutions, fostering collaboration among governments, industries, research institutions, and entrepreneurs. The transition to a circular energy economy requires more than technological breakthroughs—it depends on systems that enable the rapid development, testing, and scaling of innovations across sectors and regions. Innovation hubs, incubators, and collaborative platforms provide the infrastructure and networks needed to accelerate technological diffusion, transform business models, and align innovation with sustainability and circularity goals.

An innovation ecosystem comprises interconnected organizations and stakeholders that collectively create, support, and deploy new ideas and technologies. In the circular energy context, these ecosystems bring together diverse expertise—from renewable energy generation and digitalization to materials recovery and policy design—to develop integrated solutions. They serve as spaces where startups, established companies, universities, and public agencies collaborate to address system-wide challenges such as energy efficiency, waste reduction, and resource optimization. By fostering cross-sectoral interaction, innovation ecosystems help bridge the gap between research and practical implementation.

Innovation hubs and incubators are key components of these ecosystems. They provide startups and small enterprises with the resources, mentorship, and facilities needed to transform ideas into viable technologies or services. Hubs focused on circular energy solutions often emphasize areas such as energy storage, grid flexibility, waste-to-energy systems, and digital optimization tools. Incubators help early-stage ventures test their innovations under real-world conditions, refine business models, and connect with investors. Many of these hubs operate in partnership with public institutions, ensuring alignment with regional sustainability priorities and access to public funding or policy support.

Collaborative platforms play a crucial role in facilitating knowledge exchange and coordination among participants in innovation ecosystems. These platforms, both physical and digital, enable stakeholders to share data, best practices, and technical expertise. In the energy sector, open-access databases and online collaboration tools support the dissemination of renewable technology research, lifecycle assessment methodologies, and resource management strategies. Collaborative networks such as clean energy clusters and public-private research alliances pool expertise to solve common challenges, reducing duplication of effort and accelerating progress. This interconnectedness ensures that successful innovations spread quickly across industries and geographies.

Technological diffusion within circular energy systems involves the transfer and adoption of innovations across markets, sectors, and value chains. It requires mechanisms that reduce barriers to entry and encourage replication of proven solutions. Public policy plays a significant role in facilitating diffusion by funding demonstration projects, supporting standardization, and promoting open innovation models. Demonstration projects showcase the feasibility and performance of circular technologies—such as advanced recycling plants, hydrogen production facilities, or smart grids—encouraging investment and adoption. Once validated, these models can be replicated at larger scales, supported by public procurement or targeted incentives.

Universities and research institutions are vital actors in fostering innovation and diffusion. They provide foundational research, technical training, and analytical tools that underpin new technologies. Many universities now operate innovation centers focused on renewable energy and circular economy research, partnering with industry to commercialize findings. Through living labs and pilot programs, universities test circular energy technologies in collaboration with local governments and communities, integrating social and environmental dimensions into technological design. This approach strengthens the practical relevance and social acceptance of new solutions.

Private sector participation drives innovation by translating research into market-ready products and services. Large corporations contribute through corporate innovation programs, investment funds, and collaborations with startups. Industrial partnerships can accelerate technological diffusion by leveraging existing supply chains, production facilities, and customer networks. For example, utilities and energy service companies often collaborate with technology firms to integrate AI-driven energy management systems or circular battery recycling solutions. These partnerships combine entrepreneurial agility with industrial scale, ensuring that innovations move efficiently from prototype to widespread adoption.

Digitalization enhances innovation ecosystems by enabling data-driven collaboration and open innovation. Digital platforms facilitate real-time communication among researchers, policymakers, and entrepreneurs, breaking down silos and enabling global cooperation.

Blockchain-based systems ensure transparent data sharing and intellectual property protection, while artificial intelligence helps identify emerging innovation trends and investment opportunities. Digital twins and simulation tools allow stakeholders to test system interactions and assess environmental impacts before deployment, reducing risks and accelerating innovation cycles.

Policy frameworks are essential for supporting innovation ecosystems and ensuring that technological diffusion aligns with circular economy principles. Governments can establish research and development (R&D) incentives, innovation grants, and tax credits for circular energy projects. Regulatory sandboxes allow innovators to experiment with new business models—such as peer-to-peer energy trading or waste-to-energy schemes—under flexible regulatory conditions. Regional and national innovation strategies that integrate energy and circular economy objectives ensure policy coherence and long-term investment in sustainable technologies.

International collaboration amplifies the reach and impact of innovation ecosystems. Global initiatives such as Mission Innovation, the International Renewable Energy Agency's (IRENA) Innovation and Technology Center, and regional clean energy partnerships facilitate the exchange of knowledge and promote the global diffusion of circular energy technologies. Cross-border cooperation allows countries to share resources, pool expertise, and align technical standards, fostering equitable and accelerated transitions worldwide.

Innovation ecosystems and technological diffusion underpin the transformation of energy systems from linear, resource-intensive structures into circular, regenerative networks. By connecting actors across sectors and scales, these ecosystems promote the creation and adoption of technologies that reduce waste, enhance efficiency, and strengthen resilience. Through collaboration, shared learning, and supportive policy environments, innovation hubs and platforms turn ideas into action—driving a global shift toward sustainable, inclusive, and circular energy futures.

Chapter 9: Societal Transformation and Global Pathways

Societal transformation and global pathways define the broader context for achieving a circular energy economy. Beyond technology and policy, the success of circular systems depends on collective action, shared values, and inclusive global cooperation. This chapter explores how social norms, education, and public participation drive behavioral change, while international frameworks align national efforts with global sustainability goals. It highlights the importance of equity, cultural adaptation, and collaboration across borders in scaling circular solutions. By integrating social transformation with global coordination, the chapter outlines how humanity can collectively transition toward a regenerative, resilient, and just energy future.

Social Acceptance and Cultural Change

Social acceptance and cultural change are essential dimensions of the circular energy transition. While technological innovation and regulatory frameworks provide the foundation for circular energy systems, their success ultimately depends on public understanding, engagement, and behavioral adaptation. Shifting from a linear model of energy consumption—based on extraction, use, and disposal—to a circular model rooted in efficiency, regeneration, and sharing requires deep social transformation. Awareness, education, and participatory governance play pivotal roles in shaping this transformation, fostering trust, and aligning societal values with sustainable energy practices.

Social acceptance refers to the willingness of individuals, communities, and institutions to support and participate in the transition toward circular energy systems. Acceptance encompasses three interrelated levels: socio-political, community, and market. At the socio-political level, it involves public endorsement of policies and regulations promoting circularity, such as renewable mandates, carbon pricing, or waste-to-energy programs. Community acceptance concerns local engagement with specific projects, including renewable installations, recycling centers, and energy efficiency initiatives. Market acceptance reflects consumer willingness to adopt circular energy products and services, such as smart meters, shared mobility solutions, or renewable energy subscriptions. Achieving acceptance across these dimensions ensures that the circular transition is not only technologically feasible but socially sustainable.

Public perception of circular energy systems is shaped by trust, transparency, and perceived benefits. Citizens are more likely to support policies and projects that they understand, that demonstrate tangible environmental and economic gains, and that involve them in decision-making. Transparent communication about how circular energy systems work—such as the reuse of waste heat, battery recycling, or shared infrastructure—helps demystify new technologies and counter misinformation. Visible local benefits, including job creation, cleaner environments, and lower energy costs, reinforce positive perceptions. Conversely, perceived risks, such as changes in land use or disruption to local industries, can generate resistance if not addressed through consultation and dialogue.

Education is a powerful driver of cultural change toward circular energy adoption. Integrating sustainability and circular economy concepts into formal and informal education systems builds long-term awareness and capacity. Schools and universities can incorporate energy literacy programs that teach students about resource cycles, renewable integration, and digital energy management. Vocational and professional training ensures that workers gain the skills required for emerging sectors such as renewable energy maintenance, battery recycling, and smart grid management. Public education campaigns, delivered through media and community platforms, further strengthen understanding and encourage everyday behaviors aligned with circularity, such as energy conservation and waste reduction.

Cultural values influence how societies perceive energy and sustainability. In some contexts, consumption patterns and notions of progress are closely linked to material growth and energy abundance. Promoting circular energy requires reframing these values toward sufficiency, efficiency, and collective responsibility. Community-based initiatives—such as cooperative energy projects, shared solar installations, and local repair networks—foster cultural norms of collaboration and stewardship. These initiatives demonstrate that sustainable energy systems can enhance community well-being rather than limit it. Cultural change is reinforced when circular practices become part of daily life, supported by accessible technologies and enabling infrastructure.

Social innovation complements technological innovation in advancing circular energy transitions. New forms of participation—such as citizen energy cooperatives, crowdfunding for renewable projects, and peer-to-peer trading platforms—empower individuals to become active contributors rather than passive consumers. These participatory models build ownership and trust while decentralizing energy governance. Local leadership, social enterprises, and civil society organizations can bridge the gap between policy and practice, ensuring that circular initiatives reflect community priorities and values.

Public engagement and communication are central to fostering acceptance and cultural transformation. Consultation processes that involve citizens early in project planning build legitimacy and mitigate opposition. Interactive platforms—town hall meetings, online forums, and participatory mapping tools—allow communities to express concerns, co-design solutions, and monitor outcomes. Clear, consistent messaging that connects circular energy to everyday benefits, such as cleaner air or reduced utility bills, strengthens emotional and practical connections to the transition.

Media and digital technologies play a growing role in shaping social narratives around circular energy. Social media campaigns, documentaries, and digital storytelling amplify success stories, making circular initiatives visible and relatable. Influencers, educators, and community leaders can act as trusted messengers, bridging technical knowledge with public values. Positive framing—emphasizing innovation, resilience, and shared prosperity—helps mobilize broad support and inspires collective action.

Social acceptance and cultural change are not static outcomes but evolving processes that require ongoing engagement and reflection. As circular energy systems mature, continuous dialogue between governments, industry, and citizens ensures that transitions remain inclusive and equitable. By integrating awareness, education, and participation into every stage of the circular energy journey, societies can cultivate a shared culture of sustainability. This cultural foundation transforms the energy transition from a technical challenge into a collective movement grounded in shared responsibility, resilience, and long-term vision.

Equity, Inclusion, and Just Transitions

Equity, inclusion, and just transitions are core principles of the circular energy economy, ensuring that the benefits and responsibilities of sustainability are shared fairly across all segments of society. While technological innovation and policy reforms are driving efficiency and resource recovery, the shift toward circular energy systems must also address social justice and inclusivity. A just transition ensures that no community or worker is left behind as economies decarbonize and restructure. Integrating equity into circular energy policies promotes social cohesion, strengthens public support, and enhances the resilience of both communities and energy systems.

Equity in circular energy transitions involves fair access to energy resources, technologies, and economic opportunities. Traditional linear energy systems often concentrated wealth and infrastructure in specific regions or sectors, leaving marginalized communities exposed to pollution, high costs, and limited access to clean energy. Circular energy systems provide an opportunity to correct these imbalances by distributing benefits more equitably. Policies promoting decentralized renewable generation, community-owned energy projects, and affordable access to clean technologies help ensure that all populations—including low-income households and rural communities—participate in and benefit from the energy transition.

Inclusion ensures that diverse voices and perspectives are represented in the design and implementation of circular energy strategies. Meaningful participation allows communities to influence decisions that affect their livelihoods and environments. Participatory planning processes, citizen assemblies, and local advisory boards create mechanisms for dialogue between policymakers, industry, and civil society. Inclusive governance also recognizes the importance of indigenous and local knowledge systems, which often embody principles of resource stewardship and regeneration consistent with circularity. By incorporating these perspectives, circular energy policies become more contextually grounded and culturally appropriate.

The concept of a just transition, rooted in the labor movement and later adopted by environmental policy frameworks, focuses on protecting workers and communities during economic transformation. As fossil fuel industries decline, workers in those sectors face job displacement and income insecurity. Circular energy policies must provide pathways for reskilling, job creation, and social protection. Investments in renewable energy, energy efficiency, and material recovery industries can generate new employment opportunities while supporting affected workers through retraining programs and wage transition support. Social dialogue among governments, employers, and labor unions helps design equitable labor policies that balance environmental goals with social welfare.

Regional disparities in economic capacity and infrastructure also influence the inclusiveness of circular energy transitions. Urban areas often have greater access to investment, digital technologies, and policy support, while rural regions may face barriers to participation. Addressing these gaps requires targeted interventions such as rural electrification programs, microfinance for small-scale renewable projects, and capacity-building initiatives. Decentralized systems—like off-grid solar, biogas, and micro-hydropower—empower communities to produce and manage their own energy, enhancing self-reliance and resilience. These localized solutions embody the circular principle of using available resources efficiently while supporting regional equity.

Gender equity represents another dimension of inclusion in circular energy systems. Women often play key roles in energy use, household management, and community organization, yet remain underrepresented in decision-making and technical fields. Circular energy transitions offer opportunities to promote gender equality through inclusive employment, entrepreneurship, and leadership initiatives. Training programs and financial mechanisms that support women-led clean energy enterprises not only advance equity but also strengthen innovation and community engagement. Integrating gender-responsive policies ensures that the circular economy supports both environmental sustainability and social empowerment.

Global equity must also be considered, as resource availability, financial capacity, and technological development vary widely between nations. Developing countries, which are often disproportionately affected by climate change and resource depletion, require access to finance, technology transfer, and institutional support to participate fully in the circular energy transition. International cooperation through climate finance mechanisms, development partnerships, and trade agreements can promote fair participation. Aligning global circular policies with principles of common but differentiated responsibilities ensures that transitions are inclusive and equitable across borders.

Inclusive communication and education further enhance fairness in circular transitions. Public awareness campaigns that explain the benefits of circular energy—such as reduced waste, lower costs, and job creation—build understanding and trust. Community education programs equip citizens with the knowledge to engage in decision-making and adopt sustainable behaviors. Transparent access to information about projects, policies, and funding opportunities helps prevent exclusion and ensures accountability.

Equity, inclusion, and just transitions transform the circular energy economy from a purely technical or environmental initiative into a social contract for sustainability. By prioritizing fairness, participation, and shared prosperity, circular policies strengthen the legitimacy and durability of energy transitions. A just circular energy system values both human and environmental well-being, fostering societies that are resilient, inclusive, and aligned with the principles of regeneration and long-term sustainability.

Global Cooperation and Knowledge Sharing

Global cooperation and knowledge sharing are indispensable for scaling circular energy solutions and achieving a sustainable global energy transition. The shift from linear, resource-intensive systems toward circular models of efficiency, regeneration, and resilience requires coordinated action across borders. Energy systems are deeply interconnected—technologically, economically, and environmentally—making international collaboration essential to align policies, harmonize standards, mobilize finance, and accelerate innovation. Through multilateral institutions, transnational networks, and global agreements, countries and organizations exchange expertise, share resources, and collectively advance the principles of the circular energy economy.

International institutions provide the strategic frameworks and governance mechanisms necessary for promoting global cooperation in circular energy transitions. Organizations such as the United Nations (UN), the International Energy Agency (IEA), the International Renewable Energy Agency (IRENA), and the World Bank facilitate dialogue, set shared objectives, and support implementation across member states. The UN's 2030 Agenda for Sustainable Development, particularly Sustainable Development Goals (SDGs) 7, 9, 12, and 13, establishes the foundation for integrating energy access, industry innovation, responsible consumption, and climate action into circular energy strategies. IRENA, in particular, plays a critical role by providing policy guidance, technical assistance, and data on renewable and circular technologies, helping countries align their national strategies with global sustainability targets.

Multilateral environmental agreements also serve as key vehicles for embedding circularity into energy governance. The Paris Agreement on climate change, adopted under the UN Framework Convention on Climate Change (UNFCCC), promotes global cooperation in reducing greenhouse gas emissions and enhancing resilience. Circular energy systems contribute directly to these objectives by improving resource efficiency, promoting renewable integration, and reducing lifecycle emissions. Similarly, the Basel Convention on hazardous waste management and the Minamata Convention on mercury establish frameworks that guide the responsible handling of materials used in energy systems, such as batteries and electronic waste. These agreements ensure that the environmental gains from renewable energy deployment are not offset by resource mismanagement or pollution.

Knowledge sharing and capacity building are vital for ensuring that circular energy principles are effectively implemented across different contexts. Many developing and emerging economies face challenges such as limited technical expertise, data gaps, and inadequate institutional capacity. International cooperation bridges these gaps through technical training, knowledge platforms, and research partnerships. Programs coordinated by entities like the Global Green Growth Institute (GGGI), the United Nations Industrial Development Organization (UNIDO), and the Green Climate Fund (GCF) provide technical assistance, funding, and policy support to countries adopting circular and renewable energy systems. These initiatives help build local capacity for managing energy transitions while aligning them with broader development goals.

Global research and innovation networks further accelerate technological diffusion. Collaborative initiatives such as Mission

Innovation and the Clean Energy Ministerial encourage joint research and development on clean and circular technologies. By pooling resources and expertise, participating countries can reduce duplication, share risks, and speed up the commercialization of innovations. Knowledge-sharing platforms—such as IRENA's Knowledge Hub, the UNFCCC Technology Mechanism, and regional energy observatories—disseminate best practices, data, and analytical tools that guide policymakers and industry leaders. Open-access databases and virtual collaboration spaces enable continuous learning and cross-regional exchange, ensuring that successful circular energy models can be replicated globally.

Finance and investment also rely heavily on international cooperation. The transition to circular energy systems demands substantial capital, particularly in developing regions. Global financial institutions and climate funds play an essential role in mobilizing resources, de-risking private investment, and supporting large-scale infrastructure projects. Instruments such as green bonds, blended finance, and concessional loans enable developing countries to deploy renewable technologies, build recycling facilities, and strengthen grid infrastructure. International financial frameworks ensure that funding flows align with sustainability principles, prioritizing projects that enhance resource efficiency and circularity.

Regional cooperation complements global efforts by fostering context-specific strategies and cross-border synergies. Initiatives such as the European Union's Circular Economy Action Plan, the African Renewable Energy Initiative, and the Association of Southeast Asian Nations (ASEAN) Plan of Action for Energy Cooperation illustrate how regional frameworks can harmonize standards, coordinate investments, and facilitate trade in clean technologies. Regional power pools and shared resource management systems, such as the Nordic electricity market or the Southern African Power Pool, enhance efficiency by allowing countries to balance renewable supply and demand collectively. These models demonstrate how cooperation at multiple levels strengthens both energy security and circular performance.

Public-private partnerships at the international level further drive the global diffusion of circular energy solutions. Collaborative alliances involving governments, corporations, and non-governmental organizations (NGOs) pool knowledge, technology, and financial resources. Examples include the Global Battery Alliance, which promotes responsible supply chains for critical materials, and the Renewable Energy and Energy Efficiency Partnership (REEEP), which supports market development in emerging economies. These partnerships demonstrate how shared governance structures and joint action can translate global sustainability objectives into practical outcomes.

Equitable participation and inclusivity are critical to ensuring that global cooperation benefits all nations. Knowledge sharing must prioritize accessibility, recognizing disparities in technological capability and financial capacity. South-South and triangular cooperation frameworks—linking developing countries with emerging and developed economies—promote mutual learning and adaptation of solutions to local conditions. Transparent data sharing, open technology access, and fair intellectual property arrangements foster trust and encourage wider participation.

Global cooperation and knowledge sharing form the connective tissue of the circular energy transition. By coordinating action across borders, harmonizing policies, and disseminating innovation, international institutions and networks amplify the effectiveness of national and regional efforts. The exchange of knowledge and resources transforms isolated initiatives into a collective global movement toward sustainability. In an interconnected world, the success of circular energy systems depends not on individual actors but on the shared commitment of the global community to build an equitable, regenerative, and resilient energy future.

Measuring Progress Toward Circular Energy Goals

Measuring progress toward circular energy goals requires robust indicators and monitoring systems that capture both environmental and socio-economic outcomes. As nations and industries transition from linear energy systems to circular models centered on efficiency, regeneration, and sustainability, clear metrics are essential to assess performance, guide decision-making, and ensure accountability. Monitoring progress involves not only quantifying renewable deployment or waste reduction but also evaluating systemic change—how resources circulate within the economy, how technologies extend product lifespans, and how institutions align policies with long-term sustainability objectives.

Indicators for circular energy systems span multiple dimensions, including energy efficiency, material circularity, carbon intensity, and social inclusion. Energy efficiency indicators track improvements in how energy is produced, distributed, and consumed. These include metrics such as energy intensity (energy use per unit of GDP), renewable energy share in total consumption, and grid losses. Efficiency metrics reveal the extent to which energy systems are decoupling economic growth from resource use, a core goal of circularity. Material circularity indicators, on the other hand, measure how effectively resources are recovered and reused within the energy sector. These include recycling rates for materials like lithium, cobalt, and steel used in energy infrastructure, as well as indicators assessing the proportion of secondary materials in production.

Lifecycle-based indicators provide insights into the overall sustainability of energy technologies. Life Cycle Assessment (LCA) methodologies quantify environmental impacts—such as greenhouse gas emissions, resource depletion, and pollution—across production, use, and end-of-life stages. Applying LCA consistently enables policymakers and businesses to compare technologies, identify trade-offs, and prioritize circular design strategies. Complementary metrics, such as the Circular Material Use Rate (CMUR), assess the share of materials recycled and reintroduced into the economy, providing a snapshot of resource efficiency within the broader energy system.

Carbon intensity and emissions reduction remain central indicators for tracking circular energy performance. Measuring emissions across value chains helps evaluate how circular measures contribute to climate goals. For instance, extending equipment lifespans, recycling materials, and using renewable inputs reduce the embodied carbon of energy systems. Carbon accounting frameworks, aligned with international standards such as the Greenhouse Gas Protocol, allow organizations and governments to report emissions comprehensively, including those linked to production, transport, and disposal. Indicators like carbon footprint per unit of energy produced or avoided emissions from recycling highlight the climate benefits of circularity.

Social and economic indicators complement environmental metrics by capturing the inclusiveness and fairness of circular energy transitions. These include employment creation in renewable and recycling industries, gender equality in workforce participation, and equitable access to clean energy services. Measuring job quality, training availability, and local participation in circular projects provides insight into how transitions contribute to social well-being. Economic indicators, such as investment in circular energy innovation and the value of recovered materials, reflect the growing contribution of circular systems to sustainable growth.

Monitoring progress requires integrating these indicators into coherent frameworks and information systems. Governments and international organizations use national statistical systems, sustainability reporting platforms, and digital dashboards to collect and analyze data. Harmonized methodologies ensure comparability across regions and sectors. For example, the European Union's Circular Economy Monitoring Framework and the OECD's Green Growth Indicators provide standardized approaches to measuring resource efficiency and circularity. Linking circular energy indicators with climate and development metrics ensures policy coherence and helps track contributions toward global commitments such as the Paris Agreement and the SDGs.

Digitalization enhances monitoring capabilities by enabling real-time data collection and analytics. Smart meters, sensors, and IoT devices generate granular information on energy consumption, system performance, and material flows. Blockchain technology ensures data integrity and traceability, particularly in verifying recycling rates or renewable energy origins. Artificial intelligence assists in analyzing large datasets, identifying inefficiencies, and forecasting progress. These digital tools transform monitoring from a static, retrospective process into a dynamic system capable of informing real-time decision-making.

Transparency and accessibility of data are crucial for maintaining trust and accountability. Publicly available indicators allow citizens, investors, and civil society organizations to assess progress and advocate for improvement. Open-data initiatives encourage innovation by enabling researchers and entrepreneurs to develop new analytical tools and business models. Regular progress reports and performance reviews ensure that circular energy transitions remain adaptive and responsive to emerging challenges.

Effective monitoring also requires institutional coordination. Collaboration between ministries of energy, environment, and industry ensures that data collection covers the full scope of circular activities. Partnerships with academia, international agencies, and private companies enhance methodological rigor and data quality. Establishing independent review bodies or multi-stakeholder panels can further strengthen transparency and policy alignment.

Measuring progress toward circular energy goals transforms vision into accountability. Indicators and monitoring systems provide the evidence base for continuous improvement, helping societies evaluate what works, identify gaps, and scale successful practices. By integrating environmental, economic, and social dimensions, these systems ensure that the circular energy transition delivers genuine sustainability outcomes. Continuous measurement and transparent reporting make circularity not just a guiding principle but a measurable, achievable pathway toward a regenerative and equitable energy future.

Conclusion

The circular energy economy represents a fundamental transformation in how societies produce, distribute, and consume energy. It moves beyond incremental efficiency gains toward a regenerative model that values resource stewardship, system resilience, and environmental balance. This transformation requires more than technological innovation—it demands an integrated approach linking energy, materials, governance, finance, and culture. By redesigning systems around closed loops, circularity ensures that value is retained and waste is minimized, aligning economic growth with ecological sustainability.

Central to this transformation is the recognition that energy is not an isolated sector but part of a broader web of resource flows. Circular energy systems integrate renewable generation, material recovery, and demand management into cohesive frameworks that enhance both efficiency and equity. Renewable energy decouples power generation from finite resources, while digital technologies enable intelligent coordination and transparency. Together, these innovations support an adaptive, data-driven infrastructure capable of responding to shifting environmental and social conditions.

The success of the circular energy economy also relies on institutional coordination and inclusive governance. Multi-level cooperation between local, regional, and national authorities ensures that strategies are coherent and aligned. Public-private partnerships and stakeholder collaboration mobilize resources and expertise, while international cooperation spreads innovation and harmonizes standards across borders. These institutional frameworks turn circularity from an abstract principle into a practical system of shared accountability.

Social dimensions play an equally critical role. The transition to circular energy depends on public acceptance, equitable participation, and cultural adaptation. Education, awareness, and engagement empower communities to contribute actively to sustainable change. Ensuring fairness through just transition policies helps protect workers and vulnerable populations as industries evolve. In this way, circular energy systems strengthen not only environmental sustainability but also social cohesion and economic inclusion.

Measurement and accountability ensure that progress toward circularity is transparent and verifiable. Indicators and monitoring systems enable policymakers, businesses, and citizens to evaluate outcomes and adjust strategies in real time. Data-driven governance, supported by digitalization and open knowledge exchange, provides the foundation for continuous improvement. By linking metrics on efficiency, emissions, resource recovery, and equity, these systems ensure that circular transitions remain grounded in measurable results.

The circular energy economy is, ultimately, a vision of balance—between people and planet, innovation and equity, efficiency and regeneration. It seeks to build an energy future that is resilient to disruption, inclusive in opportunity, and restorative in impact. Achieving this vision requires commitment at every level: from policymakers crafting enabling frameworks, to businesses redesigning value chains, to individuals embracing sustainable lifestyles.

As the world faces the dual challenges of climate change and resource depletion, circular energy offers a pathway to align prosperity with planetary boundaries. By rethinking energy systems through the lens of circularity, societies can create enduring value while preserving the ecological systems upon which life depends. The circular energy economy is not merely an alternative approach—it is a necessary evolution toward a future where sustainability, equity, and innovation converge to power a truly regenerative world.